Niger Delta

Niger Delta: Constraints and Pathways to Development

Edited by

Ibaba Samuel Ibaba

CAMBRIDGE SCHOLARS PUBLISHING

Niger Delta:
Constraints and Pathways to Development,
Edited by Ibaba Samuel Ibaba

This book first published 2012

Cambridge Scholars Publishing

12 Back Chapman Street, Newcastle upon Tyne, NE6 2XX, UK

British Library Cataloguing in Publication Data
A catalogue record for this book is available from the British Library

ISBN (10): 1-4438-4130-7, ISBN (13): 978-1-4438-4130-6

To my wife Grace, for her support to my career

TABLE OF CONTENTS

ACKNOWLEDGEMENTS

The initial idea for this book came during discussions at the 2010 international conference on Natural Resource, Security and Development in the Niger Delta; organized by the Department of Political Science, Niger Delta University, Nigeria, in collaboration with the Centre for Applied Environmental Research, Department of Geosciences, University of Missouri, Kansas, United States of America. Discussions in the plenary and technical sessions highlighted gaps in the literature that needed to be filled. I thank the participants of this conference for their incisive review and critic of papers that has added value to this book. In addition to giving birth to the idea for this book, three of the chapters were first presented in this conference.

I also benefited from discussions in the workshop on ''Confronting the challenges of Development, Environmental Management and Peace Building in the Niger Delta: Beyond Amnesty Programme'' organized by the Centre for Population and Environmental Development, Benin City, Nigeria, in July 2011. I particularly thank Professor Augustine Ikelegbe for his critical comments that guided my thoughts on the subject matter.

The manuscript has also benefitted from the knowledge of reviewers who provided useful comments and critics on the papers and the structure of the book. To all these persons, and my assistant, Mr. Tarila Ebiede, I say thank you.

Ibaba Samuel Ibaba

CHAPTER ONE

INTRODUCTION: INTERROGATING DEVELOPMENT DEFICITS IN THE NIGER DELTA

IBABA SAMUEL IBABA

The Niger Delta is located in the southern part of Nigeria, and has the Atlantic Ocean as its southern boundary, while it shares its eastern boundary with Cameroun (NDTCR, 2008). The geographic definition of the region lists the component states[1] as Akwa-Ibom, Bayelsa, Cross River, Delta, Edo and Rivers,[2] whereas Abia, Imo and Ondo states are included in the conception of the region as an oil-producing area (Etekpe, 2007; Tamuno, 2008; Omotola, 2010). Although oil and gas production[3] stands out as the dominant resource found in the area, it is also endowed with numerous mineral resources such as clay, gypsum, limestone, uranium, manganese, lignite, lead/zinc, bitumen, kaolin, gemstone, gypsum, feldspar, granite, glass-sand, coal, bauxite, gold, and dolomite (Sawyer, 2008: 111-115), which provide potentials and opportunities for sustainable development. Paradoxically, however, the region is one of the least developed parts in the country (Obi, 2010, p. 222). It was reported in 2008 for instance that the HDI ranking was 0.564, while life expectancy

---

[1] The federating units in Nigeria are known as States

[2] These six States make up the South-South geo-political zone of Nigeria. Nigeria is made of six geo-political zones, including the South-South, South-East, South-West, North-West, North-Central, and North-East. Each of these zones comprises between five and seven states.

[3] Oil and gas are the mainstays of the Nigerian economy, and contribute 40 per cent of Gross Domestic Product (GDP), 90 per cent of total earnings, and 87 per cent of gross national income (Akinola, 2010, pp. 55-56). The country earned US$500 billion from oil between 1960 and 2006 (Nafziger, 2008, pp. 153-154). It is also estimated that the country generates about US$4 billion annually from the export of natural gas (Obi, 2009, p. 104).

averaged 43 years. Poverty measured by income and food intake was 72.22 per cent, while access to potable water and electricity was 6.4 per cent and 34.3 per cent respectively (NDTCR, 2008; Adeyemo, 2008 p. 103; 2008, p. 69). Also in 2010, the National bureau of Statistics (NBS) listed three of the Niger Delta States (Akwa-Ibom, Bayelsa and Rivers) as States in Nigeria with the highest unemployment rates above the national average of 19.7 per cent (Fortune News, 2010). Similarly, the 2010 Nigerian poverty profile put the rates of absolute, relative, and less–than-a-Dollar-per-day measures of poverty in the six Niger Delta States of the South-South geo-political zone at 55.9 per cent, 63.8 per cent and 56.1 per cent respectively (NBS, 2012).

The literature on the Niger Delta has blamed the poor state of development on such factors as: inequity in oil wealth distribution due to the country's centralized federalism, the politicization of revenue allocation and the resultant neglect of the region's development; oil-induced environmental devastation, the resultant occupational displacement/dislocation and the failure to rebuild livelihoods; the failure of corporate social responsibility on the part of the transnational oil corporations (TOCs); corruption which has diverted funds meant for development into private pockets; and neglect of the concerns of the poor, social infrastructure and economic services in public expenditure Naanen, 1995; Enweremadu, 2008; Ukiwo, 2009; Ibaba, 2009; Ibaba, 2011).

Whereas the views on the causes of the development plight of the region are varied, there is agreement that the poor state of development has created conditions for violence, which undermined national security and the economy (UNDP, 2006; Ibaba, 2011). The Nigerian government has responded to this with development and peace-building interventions, through the establishment of development agencies such as the Oil Mineral Producing Areas Development Commission (OMPADEC), and the Niger Delta Development Commission (NDDC). These extra-ministerial institutions were given the specific task of promoting the development of the region. For example, the mandate of the OMPADEC includes the rehabilitation and development of oil-producing communities, tackling ecological problems arising from petroleum pollution, and the provision of basic infrastructure and social amenities (OMPADEC, 1993). The NDDC has similar functions, in addition to the formulation of policies and guidelines for the development of the region, and the identification of factors inhibiting the development of the area (NDDC Act, 2000). In 2000, the government also raised the derivation principle, a criterion of revenue allocation that returns a percentage of revenue derived from mineral exploitation to the State (region) where it is produced.[4] This was raised from 3 per cent to 13 per cent, to meet agitations which blamed the manipulation of the derivation for frustrating the development of the Niger Delta. Derivation is a principal criterion for revenue allocation in Nigeria. At independence, it was 50 per cent, but was later reduced to 45 per cent in 1970, and 1.5 per cent in 1984. This reduction meant that revenue inflow into the Niger Delta was reduced, and thus the demands for its revision were intended to increase the regions share of national revenue in order to provide adequate funds for development.

The TOCs operating in the region also contributed by engaging in community development projects in the oil-producing communities. For example, the Shell Petroleum Development Company (SPDC) one of the TOCs[5] operating in the region spent various sums of US$42.6 million, US$60.23 million, US$32 million and US$53 million in 1998, 2000, 2005 and 2006 respectively on community development (Ibaba, 2007, p. 49; SPDC, 2008, p. 15). Despite these efforts, the conflicts which began as community agitations against the operations of TOCs[6] in the early 1970s, transformed into insurgency in 2005 (Osaghae, Ikelegbe, Olarinmoye, & Okhomina, 2007; Watts, 2007). Militia groups such as the Movement for the Emancipation of the Niger Delta (MEND), emerged to champion the demands of the people, and their engagement tactics which included attacks on oil infrastructure undermined oil production and endangered the national economy. Because several countries depend on Nigerian oil for their energy needs, and Nigeria is a major oil exporting country, this internationalized the impact.

The Nigerian government responded to this by instituting the amnesty programme. The 60 day amnesty which commenced on August 3, 2009, and ended October 4, 2009, offered forgiveness to combatants in return for the renunciation of militancy, arms surrender, and re-integration (Adeyemi-suenu & Inokoba, 2010). Since the amnesty programme was introduced, attacks on oil infrastructure have ceased, and oil production has risen from 700,000 barrels per day to 2.3 million barrels per day (Joab-Peterside, 2010, p. 94), suggesting that peace has returned to the region.

---

[4] In Nigeria, revenues are put into a single purse known as the federation account, and are distributed to all tiers of government each month, on the basis of criteria such as derivation, equality of states, and population

[5] Other TOCs operating in the region are Chevron, Mobil, Agip, Elf, and Texaco

[6] The TOCs were accused of being insensitive to the development plight of the people, by neglecting corporate social responsibility, and destroying the local economies through petroleum pollution without the payment of commensurate compensation for damages or providing alternative means of livelihood.

But this has been described as negative peace, "an absence of war, civil disturbance and murder", which implies that positive peace, "a condition of justice, tolerance and plenty", is yet to be achieved (Adeyemo & Olu-Adeyemi, 2010; Rivera, 2004), suggesting that violence would recur if the situation remains unchanged. Indeed, isolated attacks, claimed by the Movement for the Emancipation of the Niger Delta (MEND) in the first quarter of 2012, tends to support this. Although the Joint Military Task Force (JTF), the special intervention force in the region has dismissed the claims of MEND and blamed the attacks on few disgruntled elements, the occurrence of the attacks appear to vindicate the fears of resurgence of violence in the post amnesty era. The transformation of the conflict from one phase to another, despite the interventions by the government has elicited the concern of scholars, and researchers who have engaged in an exciting debate on the development challenges and opportunities for development in the region. This book joins this debate by presenting selected viewpoints on the subject matter.

Scope of the Book

The book is divided into eight chapters, which explore the complex constraints and pathways to development in the region. The first chapter, "Introduction: Interrogating Development Deficits in the Niger Delta", by Ibaba Samuel Ibaba, provides the background of the book and introduces the chapters which follow. This is followed by the second chapter "Challenges to Sustainable Development in the Niger Delta (Nigeria)", by Rhuks Ako, interrogates the challenges to sustainable development in the Niger Delta and locates them in the wider national context. The chapter highlights issues in Nigeria's oil-rich Niger Delta that have continued to present a sustainable development conundrum for the Nigerian government, and illustrates how these challenges have affected progress towards sustainable development. The chapter reflects on the context of sustainable development from its definitional perspectives, and provides a sustainable development framework that can enhance understanding of the challenges to sustainable development in the Niger Delta. The author suggests that the Nigerian government should adopt a comprehensive sustainable development framework for the country generally, and in particular, the Niger Delta.

This is followed by the chapter by Freedom C. Onuoha and Gerald E. Ezirim, entitled the "Resource Curse and National Development in Nigeria", and is intended to draw attention to the fact that the lack of development in the Niger Delta and the resultant conflict is part of a wider national plight. The authors review the resource curse thesis and its application to Nigeria, on the basis of the three elements of the thesis: a) natural resource abundance as a factor in internal conflict; b) natural resource abundance deepens excessive dependence on such resource (monoculture economy), making the country very susceptible to global shocks; and c) natural resource abundance engenders weak governance institution, leading to pervasive corruption and widespread poverty. The authors conclude that the resource curse is pervasive in Nigeria, and note that the Niger Delta region is one of its victims.

The fourth chapter is entitled, "Environmental Degradation and Rural Development in the Niger Delta". Authored by S. I. Efe and A. O. Abotutu, the chapter analyzes the impact of environmental degradation on the rural population, and reports that oil spills, gas flare, flooding, and erosion, have undermined rural economies and exacerbated poverty.

The fifth chapter, by A. A. Agagu, is entitled, "Nigeria, Reinventing Public Policy for the Management of Niger Delta Crises through Ethical Reorientation". The central argument of the chapter is that public policies that take the concerned people for granted, and whose formulation and implementation are devoid of ethical finesse would continue to evoke crises. The chapter sets out to examine the factors that inhibit public policy success in the Niger Delta, and proffers alternative policy options. It observes that the failure of public policy in the Niger Delta derive from many factors, including the nature and character of the Nigerian state and its federalism, policy actors, the political elites and weak public institutions.

The sixth chapter is entitled, "Budget as a Tool for Social Development: A Review Of Rivers State Capital Budget (1989-2009)", and is authored by Steve Tamuno and Titus Udom. This chapter reviews the capital budget of the Rivers State government from 1989 to 2009. The nominal, real values (discounting for inflation) and per capita budget figures for the relevant years were analyzed using various statistical tools. The authors aim at determining the efficiency of the capital allocations and the relationship of these allocations to certain social and economic indicators. The findings of the reviews and analysis show that, the sectoral allocations do not show a consistent pattern and relationship with the economic and social realities in the state. The real capital allocation to the social sector (health and education) does not show a positive relationship with population growth and total capital budget. The population of Rivers State has witnessed a rapid growth in the period under consideration due to the increasing economic importance of the state and relative peace. Unfortunately, the capital allocation to the social sector over these years does not match the population growth and its attendant pressure on social amenities. Until 2000, women and youth development was not accorded special attention in capital allocation. There must be a conscious effort to link capital budgeting to the social and economic indicators like population distribution, urbanization, unemployment, youth and gender balances. To achieve this, the chapter insists there must be active involvement of and input from all stakeholders in the budget preparation, appropriation and execution processes.

Chapter seven of the book is authored by S. R. Akinola, L. Isidahomhen and T. A. Akinola. Entitled "Making the Commons Work in the Rural Niger Delta: The Role of Women in Stabilizing Development", this chapter uses the Institutional Analysis and Development (IAD) framework to analyze the participants' behaviour, pattern of interactions and decision-making in relation to the commons and project delivery in the Niger Delta. It also analyses the gap created by not involving women in the development process in the region. The Chapter asserts that though the associational life of women in the Niger Delta has impacted positively on their communities, they have not been accorded their rightful position in formal decision-making, where they could demonstrate their full potential towards developmental activities and community governance. In spite of the fact that the people look forward to seeing development projects completed, deep-seated insincerity, selfishness and deceit on the part of some groups—elites, some traditional leaders, chiefs, political godfathers, some youths, etc.—have dashed the hope and aspirations of the grassroots. Women, as mothers that bear the brunt of the hardship in the villages, are more 'moderate' in their 'reasoning'. They are exempted in matters of plundering and pillage. In order to make the commons work, this paper therefore argues for women's involvement in decision-making from planning to execution of development projects in the Niger Delta. In order to overcome deep-seated inequalities skewed against women participation in decision-making and development, the women should be socio-economically and politically empowered so that they can have a voice in the proposed Self-Governing Community Assembly (SGCA). Thereafter, the chapter uses the IAD framework to chart a possible course of action to empower, and integrate women into the mainstream of formal decision-making arrangements in the Niger Delta.

The final chapter, "Conclusion: Addressing Deficits in Governance: The Path to Development in the Niger Delta", by Ibaba Samuel Ibaba, provides insights into development deficits as the most fundamental cause of the lack of development and violence in the Niger Delta. The chapter draws attention to the possible role of sociopathic personality in the poor governance of the region, and calls for governance reforms that will not overlook this under-indicated theme in Niger Delta discourse.

CHAPTER TWO

CHALLENGES TO SUSTAINABLE DEVELOPMENT IN THE NIGER DELTA (NIGERIA)

RHUKS AKO

Introduction

Sustainable development is the contemporary development model that generally aims to strike a balance between economic, environmental and social issues, in order to ensure optimal living standards for the present generation without denying similar opportunities to future generations. Within this rather general description of this contemporary paradigm lie several uncertainties, not least related to its definition, scope and application. Theoretically, sustainable development is the point where the three pillars interlock. In practice, trade-offs among the three pillars are necessitated by several factors including the country's stage of economic development. The above considerations notwithstanding, the term 'sustainable development' is routinely applied, especially by bureaucrats, to describe and justify government policies, laws and activities even when prior due cognizance had not been given to the three pillars that constitute sustainable development. However, while the definitional and conceptual issues give rise to challenges in implementing 'sustainable development', the overriding consideration given to economic issues over environmental and social considerations that are equally important under the contemporary development paradigm seems to be the major challenge.

This chapter discusses the challenges to sustainable development in the Niger Delta, and is divided into five sections, including this introduction. The second section engages some of the concept's definitional issues and proffers a working definition. The third section traces the evolution of the paradigm and highlights key developments. This section complements the first section as it discusses the interaction and necessary trade-offs that must occur to achieve the goals of the concept as defined in the previous section. The fourth section reveals the prioritization of economic considerations over environmental and social issues with examples drawn from the Niger Delta region. The region that hosts oil exploration and production activities is a prime example of how the elements of sustainable development are interwoven and interact, and present a dilemma for the government to determine its sustainable development priorities. The analysis is carried out in three parts defined by the periods of global summits on the sustainable development discourse including the 1972 Stockholm Conference, the 1992 Earth Summit in Rio and the World Summit on Sustainable Development held in Johannesburg in 2002. The fifth section concludes the paper.

Defining Sustainable Development

The concept of sustainable development has become philosophically and politically attractive. It is not unusual that the concept is routinely extended as both the cause of injury and therapy whenever the destructive effects of development are recognized, especially over the past 30 years (Sachs, 1991). However, despite the philosophical and political attraction of the paradigm, it remains fraught with uncertainties including definitional and conceptual difficulties (Ako, 2008). One of the main reasons why there is so much uncertainty surrounding the concept is that there is disagreement on related issues, particularly the widely differing definitions of 'need' between rich and poor nations or, within nations, rich or poor families. This suggests that the concept of 'sustainable development' is necessarily appreciated differently among the rich and poor, be they individuals or nations. Thus, to understand the challenges to sustainable development in the Niger Delta, it is essential that the paradigm is particularly appreciated from a developing country's perspective. While this observation may seem pedestrian, it is arguably one of the most fundamental challenges to sustainable development in the Niger Delta. Indeed, without a working definition, or definitive parameters for the paradigm, it is difficult, if not impossible, to measure whether or not progress is made towards sustainable development. While numerous definitions abound for the concept of sustainable development, definitions are influenced by several factors, and are often applicable pragmatically. This section highlights some of the factors that shape and/or limit the definition of the sustainable development paradigm and thereafter, proffers a working definition that suits developing countries like Nigeria.

Sustainable development, like most concepts, lacks a precise definition, and attempts to define it fall within two broad categories: sectoral or holistic. The sectoral approach emphasizes one of the three pillars of sustainable development (the environment, economic, and social) while the holistic definitions tend to be more all-embracing. Usually, the authors of sectoral definitions are inclined towards highlighting their subject of specialty as the dominant element of the sustainable development paradigm. Thus economists such as Goodland and Ledoc (1987), Haveman (1989), Costanza and Wainger (1991), and Holmberg (1992) all define sustainable development by highlighting the economic element. The environmental element is emphasized in definitions offered by environmentalists such as Lele (1991), Winograd (1995), and Pearce and Watford (1993), while the social angle is emphasized by social scientists such as Munro (1995), Hossain (1995), and Norgaard (1992). Holistic definitions, on the other hand, are more encompassing, and tend to emphasize the overall objective of the concept, which is to attain optimal level of interaction between the three elements (Barbier, 1989). Such definitions include that proffered by the World Commission on Environment and Development, which sees sustainable development as 'the ability of humanity to ensure that it meets the needs of the present without compromising the ability of future generations to meet their own needs' (WCED, 1987: 3).

Although this appears to be the most quoted definition, it has not by any means ended the search for a comprehensive definition of 'sustainable development'. Theoretically, the goal of sustainable development is to achieve an optimal balance among its three elements with due consideration to inter-generational equity: in practice, this requires trade-offs among these elements. This implies that, in some instances, environmental considerations may have to be sacrificed for economic progress. The type and level of trade-offs will necessarily be determined by the level of economic development the country in question has achieved. Developed countries are less likely to sacrifice social and environmental concerns for economic development, while the reverse is more likely to be the case in developing countries. It is to be expected that in developing countries such as Nigeria, economic development (measured quantitatively in terms of increased food availability, real income, educational services, health care, sanitation and water supply, etc.) will be given pre-eminence in the trade-offs. Consequently, a pragmatic approach must be adopted in defining sustainable development to ensure its relevance to the society in question.

Contributing to the on-going debate on the definition of sustainable development, as well as providing a working definition of the concept to suit developing countries such as Nigeria, it is suggested that the paradigm refers to:

> Improving and maintaining the quality of life of all human beings; particularly those in less developed nations, with their active participation in the process and ensuring that the socio-economic and environmental capacities are well managed using available knowledge and technologies to ensure that future generations can have at least equivalent benefits and quality of life to those of the present generation" (Ako, 2008, p. 125).

The definition recognizes the over-arching importance of economic development in developing countries, while highlighting the need to recognize the importance of citizens' involvement and contribution to the economic development process to optimize both their capacities in the process and protect them (and future generations) from their peculiar vulnerabilities. It also suggests that technologies adopted, ostensibly to promote economic development, must be subjected to inter- and intra-generational socio-economic and environmental concerns. In concluding this definitional section, it is pertinent to note that 'sustainable development' is not constituted from a fixed set of goals, but the integration of processes (which are subject to change) whereby the exploitation of natural resources, direction of investments, orientation of technological development and institutional changes are made consistent with the needs of the present and future generations . It is therefore necessary to constantly engage with the dynamism of the concept to re-order priorities in relation to prevalent circumstances.

The Evolution of Sustainable Development

This section discusses the evolution of the sustainable development paradigm with particular emphasis on its dynamic nature. This discussion is most pertinent to buttress the point that plans and initiatives aimed at promoting sustainable development cannot afford to be static. As noted in the previous section, it is necessary to constantly re-order priorities among the three elements to emphasize contemporary challenges and plans to combat them. It appears that one of the challenges to sustainable development in Nigeria is the inability of policy makers to recognize and re-order priorities to face peculiar challenges. Instead, the assumption appears to be that economic development is, and must continue to be, the priority, to attain sustainable development. This section discusses how the three pillars of sustainable development—the environment, economic and social—became entwined on the one hand, and how the complex relationship between these elements is managed (at least, on the global level) to achieve the desired results. The need for constant trade-offs among the three elements is evident in the evolution of the concept. This section presents a timeline of global meetings that defined and expounded the sustainable development paradigm. The timeline serves as reference points in the following discussion on sustainable development in Nigeria.

The publication of *Our Common Future* (WCED, 1983) popularized the term 'sustainable development' and researches into the concept in a holistic manner. That notwithstanding, the core principles of what we understand as 'sustainable development' had been the subjects of research and publications even before the turn of the century (Ako, 2008). For instance, Malthus (1798) had published an essay that examined the principle of population, as it affects the future improvement of society. By the turn of the century the works of social scientists including Pigou (1932), Veblen (1948) and Kapp (1950) drew attention to the external costs of economic activities, pollution, loss of biological diversity, premature depletion of energy and other non-renewable resources, erosion, deforestation, as well as unsustainable social developments like widening income disparities, amongst others. Expert groups also contributed to the sustainable development discourse. The International Biological Programme (IBP), a ten-year study initiated by nations around the world in 1963, contributed to laying the foundation for science-based environmentalism through its study on environmental damage with respect to the biological and ecological mechanisms through which it occurs and the conservation and growth of natural resources for human benefit. The Club of Rome, established by 36 European economists and scientists, commissioned a study of global proportions to model and analyze the dynamic interactions between industrial production, population, environmental damage, food consumption and natural resource usage in 1968.

The Founex group emphasized the developed/underdeveloped-country dichotomy to global environmental problems in its report which noted that while concern about the environment sprang from the production and consumption patterns of the industrialized world, many of the environmental problems were a result of underdevelopment and poverty (*Sustainable Development Timeline* http://www.iisd.org/rio+5/timeline/sdtimeline.htm). The Report, which also emphasized the need to integrate environment and development strategies played an important role in persuading developing countries to attend the Stockholm Conference (1972), the first global effort that engaged in the environment/development discourse that metamorphosed to become 'sustainable development'. Also worthy of note in this era is Rawls' seminal publication *A Theory of Justice* (1971), in which he argued (based on utilitarian reasoning) that intergenerational equity was an important factor in social equity and justice. This contributed to the acknowledgement of the veracity of intergenerational concerns that currently is the core of modern-day 'sustainable development'.

These efforts raised international awareness on the intrinsic relationship between the environment and development and culminated in the United Nations Conference on the Human Environment held in Stockholm in 1972. The Stockholm Conference, which has been followed by several bi- and multi-lateral meetings on related issues, had several achievements. First, it raised global awareness on the importance of environmental considerations in economic development; and secondly, it led to the establishment of environmental agencies (international and national), and provided Non-Governmental Organizations (NGOs) with the impetus to intensify their efforts to promote the 'sustainability' agenda. One of the outcomes of the Conference was that a global meeting would be held every decade to take stock of international advancements in meeting the goals and targets set.

Whilst there was no meeting in 1982, several international efforts including the World Commission on Environment and Development (WCED) contributed to better understanding of the contemporary sustainable development paradigm. The WCED report, *Our Common Future* (1987) wove together social, economic, cultural and environmental issues that had hitherto been identified as issues affecting (sustainable) development, but not discussed holistically. The report, which asserted that economic development cannot stop, but must change course to fit within the planet's ecological limits, became the basis for a new global development orientation and instigated international consultation processes towards better understanding of the concept. The two global meetings on the discourse held subsequently have expounded the broad sustainable development paradigm while emphasizing particular elements that have gained priority in the necessary trade-offs.

The 1992 UN Conference on Environment and Development (UNCED) held in Rio developed the link between the environment and development and made significant gains in the development of international statements and agreements aimed at resolving some of the conflicting issues in the environment/development discourse. They include the Rio Declaration, which defined the rights and responsibilities of states; Agenda 21—a comprehensive plan of action to be taken globally, nationally and locally by organizations of the United Nations System, Governments, and Major Groups in every area in which human impacts on the environment; the Statement of Forest Principles—a set of 15 non-legally binding principles governing national and international policy-making for the protection and a more sustainable management and use of global forest resources; and two legally binding multilateral treaties—the Convention on Biological Diversity, and the UN Framework Convention on Climate Change—which were opened for signing. While the Rio Conference is more generally associated with further highlighting the interplay between the environment and development, it highlighted the 'public participation' dimension of sustainable development via Article 10 of the Rio Declaration.

Article 10 appears to capture the essence of the Declaration, and is perhaps the most quoted part of the Declaration. It states:

> Environmental issues are best handled with participation of all concerned citizens, at the relevant level. At the national level, each individual shall have appropriate access to information concerning the environment that is held by public authorities, including information on hazardous materials and activities in their communities, and the opportunity to participate in decision-making processes. States shall facilitate and encourage public awareness and participation by making information widely available. Effective access to judicial and administrative proceedings, including redress and remedy, shall be provided.

Simply put, national governments must have legal and institutional frameworks that promote the involvement of 'concerned citizens' in the dissemination of environmental information, decision-making and access to remedies.

A decade later, the nations of the world met in Johannesburg, South Africa for the follow-up Earth Summit, dubbed the World Summit on Sustainable Development (WSSD). While the Summit re-emphasized the three-pillared approach to sustainable development (Holder and Lee, 2007), the social and economic outcomes of the WSSD outweighed the environmental protection ones (Rajamani, 2003). Rajamani (2003) observed that other indicators of this assertion include the agenda and focus of the meeting, the media's reference to the conference as the 'World Development Summit', and that the final issue to be decided at the Summit was not an environmental issue but one on the provision of health-care services to women. Rajamani (2003) adds that the move by developing countries to consolidate the Common-but-Differentiated principle—as articulated in Principle 7 of the Rio Declaration—as the basis for international action with respect to the three pillars of sustainable development is a further indication of the shift in emphasis from environmental protection to social and economic development.

Evidently, each of the three UN meetings emphasized particular pillars of the sustainable development paradigm. While the Stockholm meeting highlighted the environmental concerns of development, Rio engaged particularly with the interplay between the environment and development, while Johannesburg highlighted poverty and human rights from the economic and social elements. The emphasis on particular elements of sustainable development at these global forums did not, and should not cast any doubts on the ambit of sustainable development which covers all three environmental, economic and social pillars. Rather, it should be seen as the recognition of the dynamism of the concept and the fluidity of the elements that necessarily interact in a bid to achieve equilibrium, if the broad goals of contemporary (sustainable) development are to be met.

Sustainable Development in Nigeria

As noted previously, most developing countries are caught in the quagmire of pursuing development sustainably, as they often sacrifice social and environmental issues for economic considerations. The oil-rich Niger Delta region is a classic and interesting case study for the following reasons. First, the region manifestly highlights the links and interaction between the three pillars of sustainable development. Economically, the Niger Delta is unarguably the most important region in Nigeria. Revenues from oil contribute about 90 per cent of total exports and at least 65 per cent of total government revenues (Budina and van Wijnbergen, 2008; US Energy Information Administration, 2010). The environmental qualities of the region include being one of the world's largest deltas and wetland areas; being one of the most extensive freshwater swamp forests in west and central Africa, as well as being the largest mangrove forest in Africa, and the third largest worldwide (Rangley, 1994 and Moffat and Linden, 1995). The social inequities in the region include oil-related human rights abuses, lack of public participation in environmental issues, and inadequate benefits from oil-revenues, amongst others (Ako, 2011).

Secondly, the region continues to present a development conundrum for the federal government. Despite the natural resources that abound in the region, it remains historically 'poor and backward' and, more recently, conflict-ridden. The federal government published the Niger Delta Regional Development Master Plan (2007) to serve as a development guideline to combat the economic, social and environmental deprivation that has resulted from the operations of the oil industry. The report outlines a holistic plan towards achieving sustainable development in the region by heralding the return of peace, enhanced productivity in the region, and an increase in oil revenue for the nation (Okereke, 2007). The federal government restated its resolve to develop the region sustainably after it initiated the amnesty programme in 2009 to combat the high rate of violent conflicts occasioned by 'unsustainable development'.

The discussion is carried out in three parts, each one representing the period beginning with the year that one of the three main global conferences that have expounded the concept of sustainable development was held. Particular reference is made to the pillar of sustainable development that was highlighted in the meeting in discussions. Thus, from 1972, advancements in the recognition of the relevance of environmental considerations in economic planning are considered: progress made regarding environmental legislation and enforcement, particularly public participation from 1992, and the situation with reference to poverty-alleviation and social inclusion since 2002. The analysis in this section is based on the development of institutional and legal frameworks that imbue sustainable development processes in the Niger Delta region.

From 1972

The major outcome from the Stockholm Summit was that environmental considerations must be acknowledged during economic development planning and activities. Nigeria, like most developing countries at that time, was engaged in rapid projects geared towards economic development without much consideration for the environmental impacts. The government invested in large-scale industrial projects including the construction of steel plants, refining and petro-chemicals, and hydro and thermal power generating plants, without due consideration for the negative social and environmental impacts of these activities (Hussaini, 1997). Anago (2002) noted that these activities left a legacy of deterioration in health quality and the generation of health hazards, pollution to environmental media and the destruction of traditional economic infrastructures within communities hosting some large-scale economic development-orientated projects.

Major developments that propelled environmental concerns into the limelight occurred in Nigeria in related events between 1988 and 1989. In 1988, a Federal Environmental Protection Agency (FEPA) was established with the overall responsibility of protecting and developing the Nigerian environment. In 1989, the Agency published a comprehensive National

Policy on the Environment (NPE) that was the culmination of conferences and meetings including the International Workshop on the Goals and Guidelines of the National Environmental Policy for Nigeria (the International Workshop) that was organized with the aid of the United Nations Environmental Programme (UNEP) (Okorodudu-Fubara, 1988). Interestingly, UNEP, which assisted with the organization of the International Workshop, was created as a follow-up to the Stockholm Conference; the International Workshop recommended the establishment of FEPA, and FEPA eventually published the outcomes of the International Workshop as the NPE. This reveals the correlation between the Stockholm meeting and Nigeria's recognition of the importance of environmental issues in the development process. As Okorodudu-Fubara (1988) noted, the International Workshop was influenced by the ideas and principles advocated by prior international conferences that espoused the principle of sustainable development in the proper management of the environment and its resources and proposed goals and guidelines towards establishing a sound background for policies, laws and institutions for environmental protection and maintenance.

The resultant NPE affirmed Nigeria's commitment to a 'policy that ensures sustainable development based on the proper management of the environment in order to meet the needs of the present and future generations'. Its main objectives were listed in section 2 to include: (a) securing for all Nigerians a quality of environment adequate for their health and well-being; (b) conserving and using the environment and natural resources for the benefit of present and future generations; (c) restoring, maintaining and enhancing the ecosystems and ecological processes essential for the functioning of the biosphere to preserve biological diversity and the principle of optimum sustainable yield in the use of living natural resources and ecosystem; and (d) raising public awareness and promoting understanding of essential linkages between environment and development, and to encourage individual and community participation in environmental improvement efforts. These policy statements are reminiscent of the outcomes of the UN Conference on the Human Environment and reiterate the assertion that the Stockholm Conference played a significant role in the development of Nigeria's policy statement on the environment. Further analysis of the NPE suggests that not only did the policy document restate that environmental protection was not antithetical to economic development, but also made reference to a substantive right to enjoy a healthy environment in paragraph (a) that was quite unheard of at the time. Furthermore, the policy document resulting from paragraph (d) recognized that individuals and communities had an active role to play in 'environmental improvement efforts'.

In addition to the suggestion that FEPA be established, the NPE recommended that laws be promulgated to ratify international treaties on the environment to make them part of national law; and the establishment of a Federal Ministry of Environment, in due course, in recognition of the overriding importance of the environment in the life of the nation. While some of the objectives listed in the National Policy on the Environment were met (and highlighted in the following section), the major drawback at the time was that none of the broad aspirational statements contained therein on the protection and maintenance of Nigeria's environmental resources were legally enforceable against the State.

FEPA made reasonable strides in developing a legal framework to promote environmental protection in Nigeria. In addition to the publication of the NPE, the Agency made several other regulations to protect the environment. They included the National Environmental Protection (Effluent Limitation) Regulations, National Environmental Protection (Pollution Abatement in Industries and Facilities Generating Wastes) Regulations, and the National Environmental Protection (Management of Solid and Hazardous Wastes) Regulations. Others included the Harmful Wastes (Special Criminal Provisions, etc.) Act of 1988 (Harmful Wastes Act); the Environmental Guidelines and Standards for the Petroleum Industry in Nigeria (EGASPIN) 2002, published by the Department of Petroleum Resources (DPR); and the Environmental Impact Assessment Act. Despite these and other laudable achievements, the Agency faced several challenges that hindered the achievement of its broad objective to elevate the status of environmental consideration in the development process (Adegoroye, 1994). The obstacles the Agency faced included inadequate manpower and facilities; underfunding; the overbearing influence of individuals and groups whose activities contravene laws and regulations; and the conflicting roles among government agencies on their authority and responsibilities (Emeseh et al., 2010; Emeseh, 2006; and Adegoroye, 1994). One may argue that with particular reference to the oil industry, environmental issues continued to be sacrificed to reap maximal economic benefits. The judicial feeling expressed in *Allan Iron V Shell B-P Development Co. (Nigeria) Limited*[1] that the economic benefits of the oil industry must have pre-eminence seemed representative of the 'judicial posture' during this period (Uwais, 2002: 1).

---

[1] Unreported Suit No. W/89/71 (Warri High Court) November 26, 1973.

From 1992

The 1992 Rio Conference, as noted previously, developed the links between the environment and development, and emphasized the notion of public participation. The Conference made significant gains in the development of international statements and agreements aimed at resolving some of the conflicting issues in the environment/development discourse. These include the Rio Declaration, which defined the rights and responsibilities of states; Agenda 21—a comprehensive plan of action to be taken globally, nationally and locally by organizations of the United Nations System, Governments, and Major Groups in every area in which human impacts on the environment; the Statement of Forest Principles—a set of 15 non-legally binding principles governing national and international policy-making for the protection and a more sustainable management and use of global forest resources; and two legally binding multilateral treaties—the Convention on Biological Diversity (CBD) and the UN Framework Convention on Climate Change (UNFCCC). It is worthy of note that Nigeria developed the requisite institutional and legal framework to achieve these objectives. Its commitment to Agenda 21 is witnessed by the country's signing of the CBD and UNFCCC in 1992, and ratification in 1994. This section will, however, examine how the notion of public participation was achieved in more detail. Article 10 of the Rio Declaration states:

> Environmental issues are best handled with the participation of all concerned citizens, at the relevant level. At the national level, each individual shall have appropriate access to information concerning the environment that is held by public authorities, including information on hazardous materials and activities in their communities, and the opportunity to participate in decision-making processes. States shall facilitate and encourage public awareness and participation by making information widely available. Effective access to judicial and administrative proceedings, including redress and remedy, shall be provided.

Interestingly, Section 4 of Nigeria's NPE made similar commitments to promote active public participation environmental improvement efforts through 'ensuring broad public participation in consensus-building towards defining environmental policy objectives'. The main legislative framework to promote public participation in the environment/development discourse is the Environmental Impact Assessment (EIA) Act, whose main is to identify the environmental, social and economic impacts of a project prior to decision-making. EIAs provide an avenue to enable members of the public access to information on the state of their environment and participate in the decision-making process on activities that have the potential to adversely affect it (Kiss and Shelton, 2000 and Priscolli, 1997).

This section analyses the Act's provisions regarding public participation in activities where EIAs are mandatory. This includes oil exploration and production activities which are used specifically to highlight the effectiveness of the laws and judicial attitude. Section 23 of the EIA Act provides that:

> Where the Agency is of the opinion that a project is described in the mandatory study list, the Agency shall:
>
> (a) Ensure that a mandatory study is conducted, and that a mandatory study report is prepared and submitted to the Agency, in accordance with the provisions of this Decree; or
>
> (b) Refer the project to the Council for a referral to mediation or a review panel in accordance with Section 25 of this Decree.

Section 4 of the Act states that the 'mandatory study report' must comprise:

> (a) A description of the proposed activities;
>
> (b) A description of the potential affected environment, including specific information necessary to identify and assess the environmental effect of the proposed activities;
>
> (c) A description of the practical activities, as appropriate;
>
> (d) An assessment of the likely or potential environmental impacts of the proposed activity and the alternatives, including the direct or indirect, cumulative, short-term and long-term effects;
>
> (e) An identification and description of measures available to mitigate adverse environmental impacts of proposed activity and assessment of those measures;
>
> (f) An indication of gaps in knowledge and uncertainty which may be encountered in computing the required information;
>
> (g) An indication of whether the environment of any other State or Local Government Area or areas outside Nigeria is likely to be affected by the proposed activity or its alternatives;
>
> (h) A brief and non-technical summary of the information provided under paragraphs (a) to (g) of this section.

Clearly, this section does not expressly provide that the public be involved in the preliminary stages of the EIA process that are of utmost importance. This early (scoping) stage is considered vital to the EIA process as it provides communities likely to be affected by the proposed project the opportunity to receive information on how they are likely to be impacted and share their views (Raymond and Coates, 2002). Also, as it is during the scoping process that the terms of the EIA are negotiated and where the public is not actively involved, it is unlikely that they (the public) will actively participate in the latter stages of the EIA (Ako, forthcoming). It is important to note that, in practice, the Federal Ministry of Environment exercises its discretion to determine the level of public involvement during scoping (Ako, 2006). The Act also refers to public involvement in the EIA process in Section 7, thus:

> Before the Agency gives a decision on an activity to which an environmental assessment has been produced, the Agency shall give opportunity to government agencies, members of the public, experts in any relevant discipline and interested groups to make comment on environmental impact assessment of the activity.

However, Section 25(2) limits public participation in mandatory EIAs to comments on the conclusions and recommendations of the mandatory study report only. This provision questions the efficacy of the Act, particularly when EIAs are meant to ensure broad participation of all those that will be affected, both positively and negatively, by the proposed project. Furthermore, where a Mandatory Report is referred to mediation, or a review panel under Section 26 (a) (i)[2] or (ii)[3] of the Act, Section 37 provides that the review panel's report must contain the conclusions and recommendations of the panel relating to the environmental effects of the project and any mitigation measures or follow-up programme, and a summary of the comments received from the public.

In essence, although a summary of public comments should form part of the report, the panel need not state how these influenced its decision. Thus the law does not ensure that public comments are taken seriously and given due consideration during the decision-making process. This position, whereby public participation in the final decision-making process is limited aggravates an already deficient system where public participation is not entrenched in the early stages of the EIA process. This is emphasized by the fact that the success of EIAs is determined by the quality of their processes rather than their outcomes (Ako, 2008). In a

---

[2] Where the Council are of the opinion that the project is likely to cause significant adverse environmental effects that may not be mitigable.

[3] Where the Council are of the opinion that public concerns respecting the environmental effects of the project warrant it.

nutshell, Nigeria's EIA provisions still fall short of promoting active participation, as suggested in Article 10 of the Rio Declaration. Active (or democratic) public participation refers to the process which ensures that public opinion in the EIA process is properly considered and consequently influences decision-making (Stærdahl et al, 2003; Ako, 2006).

Oil exploration and production activities which are on the mandatory list are subject to the EIA provisions highlighted above which do not promote the active involvement of the host communities in the decision-making processes as it affects their environment. There is no gainsaying that the lax EIA provisions have contributed to the state of the Niger Delta environment which has been continually polluted by oil-related activities and widened the gulf in the relationship between the oil companies and their host communities which is fraught with mistrust. These two factors, which could otherwise be managed by a good EIA system, contribute to restiveness in the oil-rich Niger Delta region and the consequent escalation of violent conflicts in the area. Furthermore, the federal government appears to be caught in its dual role as operator and regulator of the oil industry, with its role as the former taking prominence in many instances.

For instance, FEPA did not advertise the report of Mobil's Natural Gas liquids (NGL) recovery project until a lawsuit on the propriety of the environmental assessment was initiated (Frynas, 2000). In some other instances, as exemplified by the facts in *Douglas v Shell*,[4] the mandatory EIA is not carried out, and attempts to enforce the law are frustrated. In that case, the plaintiff sued the proponents of the Nigerian Liquefied Natural Gas (NLNG) project at Bonny, which included the Federal Government and a consortium of oil companies (with Shell as operator) for failing to carry out the mandatory EIA required by law for such projects before embarking on it. The Federal High Court dismissed the case on the grounds that the plaintiff did not have *locus standi* to institute the action, despite being a native of one of the affected communities and a frontline environmental activist. According to the court, Douglas did not show prima facie evidence that his right was affected, nor any direct injury caused to him. On appeal, the decision of the lower court was held to be erroneous. The appellate court set aside the earlier decision and remitted the retrial to a different judge.[5] However, the retrial did not proceed, as the project had been completed. It is noteworthy that community problems evolved shortly after, and that the Federal Government became actively involved in assisting in the conclusion of a memorandum of understanding

[4] (1999) 2 NWLR (Pt. 591).

[5] Unreported Suit No. CA/L/143/97 in the Court of Appeal.

(MOU) between the NLNG and the community so that the first shipment of LNG would not be delayed. These are issues that could (and should) be avoided in Nigeria by having proper EIA legislation and institutional framework in place.

From 2002

As noted above, the 2002 WSSD reiterated the three-pronged characteristic of the sustainable development paradigm, but highlighted the importance of poverty alleviation and human rights issues (Birnie, Boyle and Redgwell, 2009). Nowhere is the link between poverty and human rights more apparent in Nigeria than the oil-rich Niger Delta region where, despite the enormous contribution of revenues from the oil extracted from the region to the nation's coffers, it remains historically one of poorest, and most backward and neglected areas of the country (Willinks Commission Report, 1958). The exploitation of oil resources in the region, and the deleterious impacts on the environment, highlight germane issues regarding the nexus between poverty and human rights. This section examines the extent to which the Nigerian government has attempted to alleviate poverty and improve the social status of the indigenes of the Niger Delta.

It must be stated from the outset that the environment and poverty alleviation are inextricably linked in the region where the traditional sources of livelihood are fishing and farming (UN Niger Delta Human Development Report, 2006: 37). Any real attempt to alleviate poverty must thus recognize the role of oil-related pollution in the degradation of water bodies and arable land in the region, thereby making it difficult for the region's inhabitants to earn a living and exacerbating the rate of poverty (UN Niger Delta Human Development Report, 2006: iii). The report noted that in most cases the conditions of rural communities where crude oil is produced are deplorable, with severe environmental degradation, and no access to safe drinking water, electricity or roads. The near absence of schools, health facilities, unabated gas flaring, and recurring incidences of oil spills further exacerbate the situation which contribute to the inhabitants' disillusionment, frustration about their increasing deprivation and deep-rooted mistrust (UN Niger Delta Human Development Report, 2006: iii). Analyzing the above human development issues in a rights-based context leads to the conclusion that the inhabitants of the Niger Delta have been (and are) deprived of their rights to environment, health, property, family life, development, and economic sustenance in the course of oil exploitation. In other words, although oil may have contributed to the development of the country, it has neither impacted the economic and human development of the region positively, nor contributed to its sustainable development. This is apparent as economic indices for the region remain low, the environment continually degraded, and social factors, particularly human rights, arguably the worst in the country.

The government's response to the state of affairs in the Niger Delta in this regard has been typical. Development boards, including the Niger Delta Development board (NDDB), the Oil Minerals Producing Areas Development Commission (OMPADEC) and, most recently, the Niger Delta Development Commission (NDDC), have been set up at different times to 'speedily develop the region'. Evidence in the region supports the assertion that none of these organizations has achieved its core targets. If anything, the general situation in the region worsened because the inhabitants of the region became further frustrated with the ineptitude of the organizations that were established primarily to better their lives. Consequently, they became more pro-active in their opposition to the oil industry, and with the proliferation of arms the conflicts became increasingly violent. While the government has temporarily curbed militancy in the region with its amnesty initiative, it is poised to achieve sustainable development goals in the Niger Delta by implementing the Niger Delta Regional Development Master Plan (2006).

In a nutshell, the Master Plan is touted to be a comprehensive analysis of the life development imperatives, challenges and opportunities in the Niger Delta, which puts into perspective the economic growth; human and community needs, institutional development, physical infrastructure and natural environment of the region. This plan includes twenty-five sectors, including baseline and demography, education, health, environment and hydrology, biodiversity and natural resources and financial instruments among others, and topic-specific studies into conflict impact assessment, poverty reduction, community development and governance, HIV/AIDS and youth unemployment. While the Master Plan undoubtedly captures the rhetoric of 'sustainable development', it is doubtful that the government has taken any firm steps towards actualizing the lofty goals therein. Since the federal government succeeded in reducing the rate of militancy in the region, it seems to be concentrating its efforts on the promise to provide infrastructural development on the erroneous basis that provision of such infrastructure is tantamount to sustainable development.

Undoubtedly, the provision of these amenities may bring benefits the region, but they can only be optimized where the indigenes of the Niger Delta are empowered to be economically independent. Genuine plans and actions regarding environmental remediation and protection should be a priority, given the reliance of the indigenes of the region on their natural environment for economic sustenance. Indeed, social exclusion in the region is either instigated and/or exacerbated by environmental factors, particularly access to land (Ako, 2011). One may ask about the relevance of rural electrification projects and road networks where there are no products to be stored and/or transported—in other words, the provision of infrastructure is not an end but a means to facilitating economic growth. The government should be seen to pay more than lip service to the amendment of environmental regulations and the commitment to ensure that oil operations give due consideration to the environment. The recent amendment to the law on gas flaring that has once again postponed the end-date for gas flaring till 2012 once again shows the government's insensitivity to the environmental plight of the Niger Delta. Although the government has increased the fines payable by oil companies that continue to flare gas on fields where exemptions have not been permitted, the revenue derived is paid to the federal government. In other words, the amended law has increased the economic benefits that will accrue to the government from gas flaring, while the environmental hazards are permitted to befall the inhabitants of the region.

While such action questions the government's sincerity to preserve the environment of the Niger Delta, allegations that the federal government meddles in the judicial process to deter aggrieved litigants from enforcing their environmental rights cast further doubts on the government's sincerity with regard to protecting the environment and uplifting the social inclusion of host communities. In *Gbemre v. Shell Petroleum Development Company*,[6] where a Federal High Court held that gas flaring was unconstitutional and a crime (especially as the Defendants did not have a Ministerial Certificate to permit gas flaring from the field in question), the federal government has been accused of meddling in the judicial process to frustrate the enforcement of the decision and appeal procedure (Friends of the Earth, 2007). When the plaintiff's representatives appeared in court at the expiration a 'stay of execution' that had been ordered earlier by Justice Nwokire, they discovered that the judge had been removed from the case, having been transferred to another court in Katsina, and the court file was not available. Similarly, at the Court of Appeal's hearing on Shell and NNPC's jurisdiction appeal, it was discovered that the case had been wrongly adjourned by court staff without any notice to the applicant or his lawyers. Reacting to these events Roderick, co-Chairman of the Climate

[6] Suit No. FHC/B/C/153/05 delivered on 14 November, 2005.

Justice Programme that is taking an active role in pursuing the case commented on the role of the government in frustrating the case thus:

> ... The fact that the judge has been removed from the case, transferred to the north of the country, and there have been problems with the court file for a second time, suggests a degree of interference in the judicial system which is unacceptable in a purported democracy acting under the rule of law (friends of the Earth, 2007).

This observation reflects the thinking of the general public that the State has neglected its responsibility to protect the socio-economic rights of the populace in order to derive maximal economic benefits from oil extraction.

Conclusion

This chapter has discussed the challenges to sustainable development in the Niger Delta. It highlighted three main issues including the lack of a proper definition, understanding and application of the sustainable development paradigm. The discussion highlighted issues in Nigeria's oil-rich Niger Delta that have continued to present a sustainable development conundrum for the Nigerian government to illustrate how these challenges have affected progress towards sustainable development. It is important that the federal government adopt a comprehensive sustainable development framework for the country generally, and the Niger Delta in particular. This entails a detailed study on the concept, and what it means for Nigeria given its peculiar complexities. As noted, only a pragmatic approach will yield dividends in the pursuance of its ideals. So far, Nigeria's purported application of the paradigm has resulted in the serious long-term environmental harm and a lack of material benefits for those most adversely affected, which is considered as the most obvious characteristics of unsustainable development (Birnie, Boyle and Redgwell, 2009:274; and Akpan and Akpabio, 2003).

CHAPTER THREE

RESOURCE CURSE AND NATIONAL DEVELOPMENT IN NIGERIA

FREEDOM C. ONUOHA AND GERALD E. EZIRIM

Introduction

> *As has frequently been underlined by pivotal studies of the so-called resource curse thesis, Nigeria seems to be a prime example of the curse that natural resources can bring* (Mahler, 2010:1).
>
> *The natural resource curse is not a destiny. The challenge, at both the national and international levels, is to adopt policies that better harness this potential* (Bannon and Collier, 2003:11).

The above apt expressions inform to a large extent not only a starting point for framing the problematique of this discourse, but also capture both the present state of underdevelopment in Nigeria and the potential for future development. As Luong and Weinthal (2006:241) have noted, "The proposition that abundant mineral resources are more often a curse than a blessing, particularly for developing countries, is by now so familiar that it has become doctrine". Indeed it seems strange, at first glance, that free endowment of valuable resources granted by nature to a country could be regarded as the reason for its misfortune. However, as often happens in the economic system, so many indirect negative effects can accompany the direct positive effects of additional wealth that the overall consequences of the abundance of natural resources on the economy can be judged as unfavourable when measured on the basis of a country's development indices.

Nigeria is a country with enormous potential for growth and development. With a population of over 150 million, Nigeria is Africa's most populous country, and has one-sixth of the world's black people. It is the eighth largest oil producer, and has the sixth largest deposit of natural gas in the world. Coupled with the possession of over 100 tertiary institutions producing more than 200,000 graduates per annum (Soludo, 2006:10), the country is blessed with abundant natural resources and human capital critical for national development. As noted by the African Peer Review Mechanism (APRM, 2008:8), "The country has the potential to build a prosperous economy, reduce poverty significantly, and provide the basic social and economic services its population needs". With the deluge of petrodollars from its expanding oil and gas industry, the expectation is that Nigeria should rank as one of the developed countries of the world.

Unfortunately, Nigeria ranks 158th out of 182 countries covered in the 2007 UNDP Human Development Index (UNDP, 2009:201). Despite its plentiful resources and unprecedented wealth generated through the sale of crude oil over the last four decades, Nigeria's potential remained largely untapped, and is at best grossly mismanaged. The majority of its population wallows in abject poverty, and unemployment is growing. The result is that the country has been caught between affluence and affliction. A common but often difficult to resolve puzzle then becomes: why does a resource-rich country like Nigeria rank among the poor countries of the world? This paradoxical situation has been explained by scholars by the 'resource curse' thesis. This denotes a perfect case of 'how a nation's wealth can make it poor'.

Against this backdrop, this chapter proceeds from the resource curse theory, whose proponents argue that extraction of resources lowers the wealth of a country unless the funds generated are invested in other forms (Stiglitz, 2005; Karl, 2005; Ezirim, 2010a). Firstly, it conceptualizes the term 'national development', before proceeding to chart the epistemic context of the resource curse thesis. This is followed by a discourse on the empirical approximations of the key postulations of the resource curse thesis in the Nigerian context. The succeeding section recommends measures that could help turn Nigeria's resource curse to resource blessing, to realize its development potentials. The chapter ends with a conclusion.

The Concept of [National] Development Explained

To better appreciate the idea of 'national development' as used in this chapter, it is logical to begin with the meaning of 'development'. The term 'development' has been variously conceptualized by scholars and writers. We do not wish to add to the proliferation of definitions, but would limit ourselves to those offered by Rodney (1972) and Nnoli (1981) as an inroad to gaining a shared understanding of the term *national development*. According to Rodney (1972), development in human society is a many-sided process that occurs at three levels: individual, social group, and society. At "the level of the individual, it implies increased skill and capacity, greater freedom, creativity, self-discipline, responsibility and material well-being" (Rodney, 1972:9). Although some of these are virtually moral categories and are difficult to evaluate, what is indisputable is that the achievement of any of these aspects of personal development is very much tied with the state of the society as a whole. They argue that:

> [A] Society develops economically as its members increase jointly their capacity for dealing with the environment. This capacity for dealing with the environment is dependent on the extent to which they understand the laws of nature (science), on the extent to which they put that understanding into practice by devising tools (technology), and on the manner in which work is organized (Rodney, 1972:10).

While Rodney views development from a layered perspective, the definition offered by Nnoli (1982) understands development from a mutually dialectical and transformative process. According to Nnoli (1982:36):

> Development is a dialectical phenomenon in which the individual and society interact with the physical, biological and interhuman environment transforming them for their own betterment and that of humanity at large and being transformed in the process. The lessons learned and the experiences gained in this process are passed on to future generations, enabling them to improve their capacities to make further valuable changes in their interhuman relations and their ability to transform nature.

The insight gained from the above conceptualizations is that development is *human-centred* rather than *artefacts-centred*; is a dynamic process rather than a static state; involves a complex interactive relationship between/among individuals and society; and is predicated essentially on *production* rather than on *consumption* (Onuoha, 2010a: 120). Viewed from this perspective, national development could therefore be defined as the unending process of qualitative and quantitative transformation in the capacity of a country to organize the process of production and distribution for the material benefits of society in a manner that sustains improvement in the wellbeing of its individual members in order to enhance their capacity to realize their full potentials, in furtherance of the positive transformation and sustenance of their society and humanity at large (Onuoha, 2010a:120). National development is thus an ensemble of sustained improvement in the political, social, economic, health, and environmental aspects of any organized political society in a manner that is beneficial to individual members of the society so that they fully contribute to the objectives of society, now and in the future, while maintaining the natural environment that sustains life on earth.

In this way, national development has various dimensions in a society. The political variables of national development include the level of political stability, the fairness and freedom of the electoral process, the representativeness of political institutions, and respect for human rights, among others. The economic parameters include the gross national product, the nature of income distribution, and pattern of resource management. The social dimension will capture gender equality, social justice, and the living standard of the citizens, including access to social services like water, education, security, electricity, and roads. The environmental aspect reflects the character of resource exploitation, the nature of environmental degradation, and the level of environmental awareness among the citizens. Having conceptualized the term 'national development', it is pertinent to examine the theoretical propositions of the resource curse thesis which guides the succeeding analysis in this chapter.

The Discovery of Oil in Nigeria

Before proceeding to the ramifications of the 'oil curse' on Nigeria's development, it is appropriate to provide the origin and the place of the oil industry in the Nigerian economy. Nigeria operates a monocultural economy that heavily depends on the oil industry for survival. The oil industry in Nigeria emerged about fifty years ago when oil was first discovered in Oloibiri in 1956, in the present day Bayelsa State of the Niger Delta region. Since the first shipment of crude oil in 1958, the Nigerian oil industry has witnessed steady growth and expansion. From a miniature infrastructural base in the early sixties, the industry now represents a vast domestic industrial infrastructure: more than 600 oil fields (60 per cent of these oil fields are on-shore, while the remaining 40 per cent are offshore), 5,284 wells, 10,000 kilometres of pipelines and flow lines, 10 export terminals, 22 petroleum storage depots, 275 flow stations, 10 gas plants, four refineries, and massive liquefied natural gas projects (Smith 2006). The Pipeline and Product Marketing Company (PPMC), a subsidiary of Nigerian National Petroleum Corporation (NNPC), uses a network of oil pipelines to transport crude oil to the refineries in Port Harcourt (I and II), Warri and Kaduna. The multi-product pipelines are used to move products from the refineries/import-receiving jetties to the 22 petroleum storage depots all over the country.

As at 2004, it was estimated that Nigeria has proven oil reserves of 32 billion barrels, while the natural gas reserves are estimated at 174 trillion cubic feet. Nigeria's oil reserves are expected to last for 37 years, while gas reserves will last 110 years (NPC, 2004:3). The Nigerian government's plan is to raise the reserves from the present level of about 36 billion barrels in 2006 to 40 billion barrels by 2010, and increase production capacity from the faltering 2 million barrels per day (bpd) to about 4.5 million bpd. The idea is to stabilize Nigeria's position as Africa's largest exporter of oil following years of intermittent attack on the oil industry by aggrieved Niger Delta militants (Onuoha, 20010b).

The industry, which is based principally in the Niger Delta, is today the mainstay of Nigeria's economy, accounting for some 80 per cent of government revenue, 95 per cent of foreign exchange earnings, 40 per cent contribution of GDP, but only four per cent of employment (Tell, 2008:33). Since the discovery of oil in commercial quantity in the 1950s, and consequent export to international markets, the Nigerian economy has continued to rely on oil exports to run the machinery of government.

Resource Curse: Theoretical and Epistemic Contexts

The general proposition that abundance of natural resources is more often a curse than a blessing, particularly for developing countries like Nigeria, is now a given. Natural resources covers "land, water, the environment and all material objects, natural or synthetic, found on and below the land, in and beneath water masses and in the atmosphere, and which can be transformed to produce value" (ECOWAS, 2008:39). The natural resources that have turned out to be a curse are largely oil and hard-rock minerals, including coltan, diamonds, gold, and gemstones, among others.

According to Malomo (2008), the idea that natural resources might be more of an economic curse than a blessing began to emerge in the 1980s. However, the term 'resource curse thesis' was first used by Richard Auty in 1993 to describe how countries rich in natural resources were unable to use that wealth to boost their economies and how, counter-intuitively, these countries had lower economic growth than countries without an abundance of natural resources.

The resource curse theory has different perspectives. According to Rosser (2006), the behaviouralist perspective asserts that natural resource abundance can lead to emotional or irrational behaviour on the part of political elites, which fosters poor resource management. The rational actor perspective points to the problems caused by rent-seeking political actors in contexts of resource wealth. The state-centred theorists propose that states, which rely on unearned income, avoid developing sound economic policies or public accountability by relying on rent-distribution politics. The historico-structuralist perspective argues that natural resources can empower elites, who then influence government policies in their favour against other social groups. Finally, the social capital perspective professes that natural resources create social tensions between those who have access to the resources and those who do not, which prevents societal cooperation and enables powerful vested interests to dominate. These different perspectives of the theory show more or less that developing petro-states tend to over-reach themselves in terms of what they expect from the oil resources at their disposal, while not making efforts to utilize these resources to the optimal benefits of the people in terms of good governance and promotion of national development.

Studies by Sachs and Warner (1995, 1999a, 1999b) have established a link between natural resource abundance and poor economic growth. Accordingly, Luong and Weinthal (2006) argue that the widely accepted contention that an abundance of mineral resources and the influx of external rents generated from these resources during boom periods are to blame for the so-called 'resource curse' should be revisited. Instead, they offered a new research agenda for studying the problem of resource-rich states that shift the locus of study away from the 'paradox of plenty' to a more appropriate paradox—that the concentration of wealth impoverishes the state, whereas the dispersion of wealth enriches the state. This agenda, according to them, focuses on three interrelated issues: the structure of ownership of mineral resources, the importance of strong institutions, and the relative influence of domestic versus international factors.

In relation to oil, Yates (2009:5-6) contends that the resource curse syndrome can be described by its symptoms: oil booms raise expectations and increase appetites for spending; governments dramatically increase public spending, based on unrealistic revenue projections; booms reduce the quality of public spending and encourage rent-seeking; the volatility of oil prices hinders growth, distribution and poverty alleviation; booms encourage the loss of fiscal control and inflation, further hampering growth, equity and the alleviation of poverty; foreign debt grows faster in oil-exporting countries, mortgaging the future; productive activities unrelated to oil, such as manufacturing and agriculture, are adversely affected by the oil sector in the phenomenon called the 'Dutch Disease'; petrodollars replace more stable and sustainable revenue streams, exacerbating the problems of development, transparency and accountability; oil-based governments often rely on repression to keep themselves in power; petrodollars support authoritarian rule; and oil becomes a rationale for starting and/or fuelling civil wars (Ezirim, 2010b:100).

In the context of Nigeria, the resource curse theory links corruption to the problem of underdevelopment especially with regard to mismanagement and misappropriation of her natural resources. Ikubaje (2006) and Ezekwesili (2006) note that the nature of corruption in the Nigerian oil sector is seen to be characterized by under-utilization of taxes and royalties—bribery from the oil companies to the Nigerian National Petroleum Corporation (NNPC) and the Central Bank of Nigeria (CBN), and the discrepancies in quoted figures. As noted by Ibeanu and Luckham (2006:12-13) a state funded by revenues extracted from oil multinationals could all too easily resist accountability for its failings to its tax-paying citizens. The commercial arrangements whereby the multinationals enjoyed a free rein under the cover of state officials thus gained prominence. Ibeanu and Luckham (2006:14) further state that the problems of national and corporate governance in Nigeria became mutually and disastrously entangled and intertwined. The one feeds the other and accounts for the great corruption in the nation and in government. State regulation of the oil sector neither ensured effective responsible corporate governance, nor ensured that the proceeds of oil were invested productively.

In general, three elements or pathways are agreed on by many scholars on how natural resource abundance manifests as a curse for a state, namely: i) natural resource abundance as a factor in internal conflict; ii) natural resource abundance deepens excessive dependence on such resource (a monocultural economy), making the country very susceptible to global shocks; and iii) natural resource abundance engenders weak governance institution, leading to pervasive corruption and widespread poverty (Ezirim and Ifesinachi (2009). In the light of the foregoing theoretical propositions, the resource curse theory could be used to explain the problem of underdevelopment or retrogression in Nigeria since the discovery of oil in the late 1950s. The resource curse thesis is therefore appropriated here as a framework for appreciating the present state of underdevelopment in Nigeria: a country with enviable potentials for economic growth and development.

The Ramifications of the 'Oil Curse' in Nigeria

As noted above, the resource curse thesis unravels at least three broad effects that resource abundance could have on a state. In line with this, the present section discuses how these broad effects have manifested in Nigeria and their implications for the prospect of national development.

Resource Abundance and Economic Performance

Prior to the discovery of oil in Nigeria, agriculture was the mainstay of the nation's economy, and there was serious effort on the part of the government to ensure that Nigeria remained a very influential state among the comity of nations given its rich endowment of human and material resources. In fact, prior to the oil boom in the 1970s, Nigeria depended largely on primary commodity exports such as cocoa, palm oil, rubber, cotton and groundnut for its national income.

Following the discovery of oil in the 1960s and the oil boom in the 1970s, Nigeria neglected its strong agricultural production and manufacturing basis in favour of an unhealthy, unrealistic and uncertain dependency on crude oil. During the 1960s and 70s Nigeria grew 98 per cent of its food and was a leading global exporter of cocoa, ground nut, cotton and rubber, but the discovery of oil led to the neglect of agricultural sector (Usman, 2010). At that time, approximately 60 per cent of Nigeria's labour force earned their livelihood from farming and a significant proportion of export earnings (Anyanwu, 1997; CBN, 2000), before the shift solely to petroleum in the 1980s.

As the production and export of oil began to increase, the Nigerian economy began to witness progressive neglect and decline in the agricultural sector. Beginning from the 1980s, there was a significant shift from an agrarian economy to a dependency on petroleum production. Increasingly, Nigeria became a major oil producer, with petroleum production accounting for over 25 per cent of GDP, 90 per cent of foreign exchange and 70 per cent of government revenues (World Bank, 2007:1). Although the deluge of revenue from oil has brought about some development projects, the current state of Nigeria is not commensurate with the volume of oil revenue that has entered into government account.

Resource Abundance and Unset of Conflicts (Wars and Insurgencies)

Another key theoretical strand of the resource curse thesis is the argument that resource abundance tends to promote the likelihood of conflicts in such society. The assumption is that resource wealth tends to promote civil wars (insurgencies) through a third mechanism, by giving people who live in resource-rich areas an economic incentive to form a separate state (Ross, 2003; Collier and Hoeffler, 2002; Fearon, 2002; LeBillion, 2001; and Ezirim and Ifesinachi 2009). The data in table 3-1 below, for instance, lists nine secessionist civil wars in regions that have abundant mineral resources.

Table 3-1: Mineral Resources and Secessionist Movements: 1949 – 2003

S/No	*Country*	*Region*	*Duration*	*Resources*
1	Angola	Cabinda	1975-2002	Oil
2	Congo DRC	Katanga/Shaba	1960-65	Copper
3	Indonesia	West Papua	1969 -	Copper, Gold
4	Indonesia	Aceh	1975	Natural gas
5	Morocco	West Sahara	1975-88	Phosphates, Oil
6	Myanmar	Hill Tribes	1949-	Tin, Gas
7	Nigeria	Biafra	1967-70	Oil
8	Papua New Guinea	Bougainville	1988-	Copper, Gold
9	Sudan	South	1983 -	Oil

Ross (2003:27)

According to Ross (2003:28), these resource-inspired insurrections have several common elements. First, before the resource was exploited, people in these regions had a distinct identity—whether ethnic, linguistic, or religious—that set them apart from the majority population; second, the widespread belief that the central government was unfairly appropriating the wealth that belonged to them and that they would be richer if they were a separate state; and third, in most cases, local people bore many of the costs of the extraction process itself—due to land expropriation, environmental damage, and the immigration of labour from other parts of the country.

With respect to oil, Bannon and Collier (2003:5) argue that "the discovery of a new natural resource or a higher endowment of a known resource greatly increases the risk of conflict in low-income countries, especially if the resource is oil". In the remote and immediate political history of Nigeria, oil resource abundance has been implicated in both the 1967-70 civil war experience and the lingering petro-insurgency that plagued the oil-rich Niger Delta region in recent times. In relation to the Biafran civil war, Zinn (2005:100) draws this nexus when he asserts that "Biafra's sovereignty is the main objective and a key element of this sovereignty is control over Biafra's resources, of which the most important is oil". The protracted petro-insurgency or conflict that bedevilled the Niger Delta region following the return to democracy in May 1999 bears testimony to the observation that resource abundance has a high propensity of instigating civil wars or conflicts.

In the classical resource-curse trajectory, several factors contributed to the outbreak of petro-insurgency in the Niger Delta region. First, oil was discovered in a region dominated by minority ethnic groups. Second, successive administrations or governments dominated by the majority ethnic groups unfairly appropriated the proceeds from the oil wealth to the detriment of the minority ethnic group from whose region the oil is derived. Third, the pattern of oil extraction was patently violent and destructive of the environment and livelihood systems of the host population. Fourth, progressive neglect of the region produced a segment of deprived and disenchanted group who resorted to violent approaches to redress the situation.

Cumulatively, these contradictions contributed to the outbreak of conflicts and opened the door for criminals, gangs, warlords, and other conflict entrepreneurs to drive, sustain and benefit from the resultant conflict economy in the oil-rich region. To briefly elaborate on this, the Niger Delta is surfeited with oil. Oil from the region accounts for about 80 per cent of government revenues, yet the region is blighted with all the negative indices of human development, especially poverty. The incidence of poverty in the region is very high, with over 70 per cent living at a subsistence level in rural areas. It is estimated that about 73 per cent of the people lack access to safe drinking water, about 70 per cent of households lack electricity, 94 per cent of the population lack access to telephones, and the primary school enrolment rate is below 40 per cent (Ibeanu, 2006).

Consequently, the prevalence of poverty and deprivation amidst enormous wealth in the region generated deep grievances among the people of the region. The local people, whose environment is being destroyed and plundered as a result of oil exploitation by multinationals coupled with marginalisation by successive governments in Nigeria, resorted to armed violence, especially when peaceful agitation failed to change the situation (Ezirim, 2008). Their resistance was informed by the logic of maintaining their security of livelihood. However, the narrow definition of national security by the ruling elite in Nigeria, which is defined in terms of unimpeded process of oil exploitation to guarantee state revenue, came in conflict with host communities' logic of security of livelihood. This contradiction created the condition for conflicts. Ensuing conflicts subsequently assumed different forms, namely; conflicts between communities or ethnic groups; conflicts between communities and the oil and gas companies in the region; conflicts between youth groups and relevant authorities; and conflicts between and within militants, cults and criminal outfits (Onuoha, 2008). For instance, between 1999 and 2007, it is estimated that Nigeria lost about US$58.3 billion in revenue due to insurgency in the Niger Delta, and over 10,000 people were killed as a result of the crises (Onuoha, 2010c:379).

As conflicts unfolded and threatened the steady flow of oil revenue, the government resorted to massive militarization of the region. Individuals and groups who felt aggrieved by these developments responded to threats of insecurity and oppression by taking up arms either as a means of self-defence or for purposes that portended negative consequences for the immediate environment. In this context, armed groups spontaneously emerged as a collective outfit for providing security for communities or ethnic groups in the Niger Delta region (Abayomi, *et. al,* 2005:127). To sustain armed struggle against the Nigerian state, various armed groups relied on alliance building as well as oil theft and illegal bunkering. In this connection, illegal oil bunkering became a crucial source of funding militancy and petro-insurgency, especially in the acquisition of sophisticated weapons. The crisis in the Niger Delta therefore illustrates an element of the resource curse thesis: that resource abundance has the tendency to lead to civil wars or conflicts.

Resource Abundance and Weak Governance

The third impact of resource abundance is its potential for weakening governance processes and institutions of the state, leading to widespread corruption, lack of transparency and accountability in resource management, and poor service delivery on the part of government. It is argued, for instance, that when a government gets more of its revenue from oil, minerals, and timber, it is more likely to be corrupt. A major explanation for this is the sheer volume of resource revenue that enters government coffers. As a result, government is able to absorb, and effectively track, only limited amounts of money (Ross, 2003:25). Also related to this is the volatility of resources revenues, which is often characterized by fluctuations (boom and bust) that tend to overwhelm normal budgeting procedures which often weaken state institutions (Gelb and Associates, 1998). In this way, government income becomes highly unpredictable and fluctuates with the vagaries of the price of such commodities in the international market.

In addition, the sudden deluge of revenue from such resources is known to overwhelm not only the capacity of the government to effectively monitor its inflow, but also, and more importantly, its ability to effectively utilize it in terms of providing deliverables to its citizens. The Nigerian experience since the discovery of oil unfortunately corroborates these findings. Over the past forty years, Nigeria has recorded unprecedented increases in material wealth generated from the sale of crude oil (as shown in table 3-2 below).

Table 3-2: Estimated Crude Oil Production and Revenue in Nigeria, 1958-2007.

Year	*Production (Million barrels)*	*Revenue (₦ million)*	*Year*	*Production (Million barrels)*	*Revenue (₦-million)*
1958	1.9	0.2	1999	774.7	500,000
1959	4.1	3.4	2000	828.3	1,340,000
1960	6.4	2.4	2001	859.6	1,707,600
1965	99.4	29.2	2002	725.9	1,230,900
1970	395.8	167.0	2003	844.1	2,074,300
1975	660.1	4,272.0	2004	900.0	3,354,800
1980	760.1	12,354.0	2005	923.5	4,762,400
1985	547.1	10,915.0	2006	814.0	6,109,000
1990	660.6	55,216.0	2007	880.0	6,700,000
1995	715.4	324,548.0	**Total**	**23,183.9**	**₦29.8 trillion**

Source: *Tell* (2008:28).

Nigeria would have been among the 20 leading economies of the world if the accruals had been judiciously utilized by the country's political leadership and invested in infrastructural developments such as roads, electricity, education, healthcare delivery, and piped water, among others. Rather, a greater percentage of Nigeria's oil wealth has either been misappropriated or directly looted by the leaders. For example, the Ibrahim Babangida administration (1985-1993) failed to account for the $12 billion Gulf War oil windfall. The former Chairman of the Economic and Financial Crimes Commission (EFCC), Mallam Nuhu Ribadu, has alleged that Nigerian leaders have stolen about $500 billion (₦85 trillion) within the past forty years (Onuoha, 2009: 8). A World Bank report reveals that about 80 per cent of Nigeria's oil and gas revenues accrue to just one per cent of the country's population. The other 99 per cent of the population receive the remaining 20 per cent (Akwuole, 2006:15). Consequently, it is estimated that in Nigeria, about 70 per cent of its population live below the survival line of one US dollar a day; over 5 million youths are unemployed; about 800 pregnant women out of 100,000 die during childbirth; and over 4.4 million Nigerians are living with HIV/AIDS (Akosile, 2007:52). This situation has compounded the crisis of development in Nigeria.

The main challenge here is the problem of lack of accountability in the Nigeria's extractive industry, especially the oil and gas industry that provides the nation's foreign exchange earnings. Since its establishment in 2004 as a monitoring mechanism, the Nigerian Extractive Industries Transparency Initiative (NEITI) has been crying foul over the lack of transparency in Nigeria's extractive industry, without any significant improvement since then. A notable dimension to the problem of lack of accountability and transparency in the industry is the conflicting figures in the daily quantities of crude oil purportedly sent to refineries for domestic refining against the actual volume received by the plant within the same period reviewed. NEITI Auditors have discovered that there is a serious accounting problem in the oil sector of Nigeria, and this has been occasioned by the lack of openness and transparency in government accounting practices in the oil sector vis-à-vis the quoted figures that oil companies claim to have paid to government coffers over the years.

The lack of sufficient information on activities of the Nigerian National Petroleum Corporation (NNPC) and oil revenues, leakages in tax revenues, differential accounting methods by the Federal Inland Revenue Service (FIRS) and the Central Bank of Nigeria (CBN) and leakages in Nigeria Customs Services (NCS) revenues and Federal Government and independent sources have led to more corruption on the part of the government since having sole ownership of oil resources makes it difficult for other stakeholders like civil society to monitor and publicize shoddy deals going on in the industry, often with the connivance of senior government officials.

The problem of lack of accountability in the oil industry has in turn deepened the problem of corruption in the country. This is basically because of the political economy of the Nigerian state. Nigeria is a rentier state that depends on oil revenue for running the machinery of government. Given that the state controls oil revenue, the implication is that government becomes the central mechanism for (mis)-managing the common wealth. Access to government means access to enormous wealth. Given the sociology of the resource curse, weakness in the institutional processes and structures of governance has led to the deepening of corruption. This perhaps explains why Nigeria has consistently been among the most corrupt nations of the world, as ranked by Transparency International in its annual corruption index. For instance, Transparency International rated Nigeria 134th out of 178 countries featured in the 2010 index. On a scale of 0-10, Nigeria scored 2.4 and also occupied 35th position out of 40 African countries featured in the 2010 index. Corruption is a key index of weak governance in any polity.

In a nutshell, therefore, excessive dependence on a natural resource (oil) has led to weak governance institutions and processes in Nigeria. This in turn has deepened the prevalence of corruption in Nigeria, thereby making natural resource more of a curse than blessing to Nigeria. The overall implication is that resource abundance has become an inhibitor rather than an accelerator of national development in Nigeria.

Conclusion

Natural resources are not necessarily evil. As Bannon and Collier (2003:11) have rightly noted, the natural resource curse is not destiny. The challenge, at both the national and international levels, is to adopt and vigorously implement policies and mechanisms that better harness the potential that comes with resource endowment. Nigeria has witnessed the 'years of locust' in the form of mismanagement of oil revenues that have not only led to missed opportunities to record accelerated development in the country, but has also resulted in insurgency in the Niger Delta region. However, all hope is not lost for Nigeria to achieve impressive development strides in the very near future. Much could still be achieved if the government can put in place processes, institutions and mechanism that would ensure that the country's oil wealth is judiciously utilized to underwrite national development.

CHAPTER FOUR

ENVIRONMENTAL DEGRADATION AND RURAL DEVELOPMENT IN THE NIGER DELTA

S. I. EFE AND A. O. ABOTUTU

Introduction

The environmental challenges confronting the world have raised concerns pertaining to their impact on poverty. According to Kasum (2010), this damage could reduce the productivity of the environment, if not completely extinguish the pleasure we can derive from it. The harm to the ecosystem is either caused by nature or by man. The natural ones come in the form of earthquakes, volcanic eruptions, landslides, and windstorms, etc., while the man-induced ones are flooding, acid rain, oil spillage, and soil erosion, etc.

It is estimated that over one billion people in the world are living in extreme poverty, unable to secure adequate food, shelter, clothing, healthcare, clean water or sanitation (Sachs, 2005). Eighteen million people die every year from such poverty-related causes as malaria, AIDS, and starvation (United Nations Children Fund, 2005). And climate change, for instance, threatens many species and ecosystems. Failing to mitigate global warming risks stronger hurricanes, massive droughts, loss of biodiversity, and the spread of disease; worst-case scenarios include the long-term flooding of coastal areas around the world by rising ocean tides.

In the Niger Delta, both oil-related and non-oil related environmental degradation has attracted the concern of scholars, researchers and policy makers, although the oil-related problems dominate on the Niger Delta. Oil production in the region is noted to have resulted in oil spills and gas flares that have been linked to poverty and violence (Opukri & Ibaba, 2008). Given that oil is produced mainly in the rural areas, it is discernible that the effects are greater in the rural communities. Similarly, the livelihoods of rural communities depend directly on the environment, and changes in environmental conditions therefore directly affect the rural economies. Against this background, this chapter examines the interface between environmental degradation and rural development in the Niger Delta. It proceeds by reviewing the impact of flooding and erosion.

Flooding/Erosion

Flood hazards have constituted a threat to the coastal, rural and urban inhabitants of the Niger Delta. Flood incidents, resulting in the loss of properties worth several billions of Nigerian naira (NGN) have been variously reported. Efe and Mogborukor (2010) have estimated that over NGN3 billion worth of properties is lost annually to flooding in Warri and its rural areas, and in the Niger Delta region of Nigeria the rate of inundation in the region and properties worth NGN15.1million were lost to flooding occasioned by heavy rainfall (Efe 2010). The Niger Delta could lose over 15,000 square kilometres of land by the year 2100 with a one metre rise in sea level. Moreover, it is predicted that Nigeria will lose about US$9 billion as a result of the sea level rise, while at least 80 per cent of the people of the Niger Delta are being displaced due to the low level of the region (Awosika et al, 1992; Awosika and Ajayi, 1994; Efe, 2010).

According to Uyigue (2007) and Efe (2010) many communities in the Niger Delta region, with many houses have been abandoned by their owners due to floods resulting from heavy and brief rainfall, and many more areas in the region are vulnerable to flooding. Owners of the affected houses did not anticipate the problem when their houses were being built (see fig.1b). In some of these areas, the flood resulted in soil erosion. For instance, this was observed in Abraka and Benin City. This observation corroborated those of Efe (2007) and Uyigue (2007) in Abraka and Benin City. Some residential buildings and primary school buildings in the neighbourhood have been washed away, thereby forcing the school to relocate. In the same vein, the Niger Delta could lose over 15,000 square kilometres of land by the year 2100 with a one metre rise in sea level as a result of climate change (see table 4-1). Moreover, it is predicted that Nigeria will lose about US$9 billion as a result of the sea level rise, while at least 80 per cent of the people of the Niger Delta are being displaced due to the low level of the region as result of the coastal flooding occasioned by the sea level rise (Awosika et al, 1992; Awosika and Ajayi, 1994).

Table 4-1: Total land loss (km^2) due to coastal inundation and erosion estimated from different scenarios of sea level rise

	Low Estimate					*High Estimate*			
Sea level rise (m)	0.2	0.2	0.5	1.0	2.0	0.2	0.2	0.5	1.0
Niger Delta	2,846	7,453	7,453	18, 398	18,398	2,865	7,500	15,332	18,803

Source: Awosika et al (1992)

Apart from the Niger Delta, flood hazards also cut across the entire country from Sokoto to Maiduguri; and from Ibadan to the south eastern part of Nigeria there have also been a series of flood episodes.

Oil spillage in Nigeria

Nigeria is the largest oil producer in Africa, and is now rated the tenth largest producer of crude oil in the world (International Crisis Group ICG, 2006), averaging 2.7 million barrels per day (bpd) in 2006. Since the discovery of oil in Nigeria in 1956, the country has suffered environmental degradation from oil spillage (Imoobe and Iroro, 2009). Nigeria's Niger Delta, has been identified as one of the world's most severely petroleum-impacted ecosystems (Annon, 2006). Nigeria has suffered major oil spills which have led to environmental despoliations. These oil spills usually contaminate coastal shorelines, causing severe localized ecological damage to the near-shore community. The growth of the country's oil industry, the lack of enforcement of environmental regulations, and population explosion have led to substantial degradation of the environment, especially in the Niger Delta region. Since the discovery of oil in the Niger Delta, oil spill incidents have occurred at different time intervals along the Nigerian coast. An estimated 9 to 13 million barrels (1.5 million tonnes) of oil has spilled in the Niger Delta ecosystem over the past 53 years, representing about 50 times the estimated volume spilled in the Exxon Valdez Oil Spill in Alaska in 1989 (Leschine et al., 1993; Weiner et al, 1997). Also, from table 4-2, a total of 4647 incidents resulted in the spilling of approximately 2,369,470 barrels of oil. Out of this quantity, an estimated 1,820,410.5 barrels were lost into the environment. This however indicates approximately 6 per cent, 25 per cent, and 69 per cent of total oil spilled into land, swamp and offshore environments respectively.

Table 4- 2: Oil Spills in Nigeria (1876-1996)

Years	*No. of Spills*	*Quantity Spilled (in barrels)*	*Quantity Recovered (in barrels)*	*Quantity Lost to the Environment (in barrels)*
1976	128	26,157.00	7,135.00	19,021.50
1977	104	32,879.25	1,703.01	31,176.75
1978	154	489,294.75	391,445.00	97,849.75
1979	157	94,117.13	63,481.20	630,635.93
1980	241	600,511.02	42,416.83	558,094.20
1981	238	42,722.50	5,470.20	37,252.30
1982	257	42,841.00	2,171.40	40,669.60
1983	173	48,351.30	6,355.90	41,995.40
1984	151	40,209.00	1,644.80	38,564.20
1985	187	11,876.00	1,719.30	10,157.30
1986	155	12,905.00	522.00	12,358.00
1987	129	31,866.00	25,757.00	25,757.00
1988	208	9,172.00	1,955.00	7,207.00
1989	228	5,956.00	2,153.00	3,803.00
1990	166	14150.35	2,785.96	12,057.80
1991	258	108367.01	2,785.96	105,912.05
1992	378	51,187.90	1,476.70	49,711.20
1993	453	8,105.32	2,937.08	6,632.11
1994	495	35,123.71	2,335.93	32,787.78
1995	417	63,677.17	3,110.02	60,568.15
1996	158	39,903,667.00	1,183,807.00	38,716.87
Total	**4647**	**2,369,470.00**	**549,060.38**	**1,820,410.50**

Source: Uyigue and Agho, 2007

In another vein, Opukri and Ibaba (2008:181) have noted that the Western Operations of the Shell Petroleum Development Company (SPDC) recorded a total of 115 incidents of oil spills in 2001, from which 5,187.14 barrels of oil were spilled. Of significance is the fact that only 734, 53 barrels of the spilt oil, representing 14.2 per cent, were recovered (SPDC Western Operations, Environmental Department, August 2002). Since 1989, the SPDC has recorded an average of 221 spills per year in its operations area, involving a total of 7,350 barrels annually (SPDC Nigeria Briefs, May 1995:3). Other oil multinationals also spill oil into the Niger Delta environment: for example, in January 1998, 40,000 barrels of light crude oil were spilled by Mobil in Eket (Da Costa, 1999). Furthermore, oil spill statistics show that a total of 2,796 oil spill incidents were recorded between 1976 and 1990, leading to the spilling of 2,105,393 barrels of oil (Punch, February 20, 1991:2). Three million barrels of oil were lost from 6,817 oil spill incidents between 1976 and 2001; over 70 per cent of the spilt oil was not recovered (UNDP, 2006:181). The World Bank (1995:49) has also noted that about 2,300m^3 of oil was spilled in 300 separate incidents in old Rivers (which includes Bayelsa State) and Delta States (see table 3). It was also reported in Punch, February 20, (1991:2) that a total of 2,796 oil spill incidents were reported between 1976 and 1990, leading to the spilling of 2,105,393 barrels of oil, and three million barrels of oil being lost to 6,817 oil spill incidents between 1976 and 2001; over 70 per cent of the spills could not be recovered (UNDP, 2006:181).

Table: 3 Oil Spills in some locations in Nigeria (1979-2005)

Locations	***State***	***Year***	***Quantity spilt in barrels***
Forcados terminal oil spills	Delta	1979	570,000
Funiwa No.5 well blowout	Rivers	1980	400,000
Oyakama oil spillage	Rivers	1980	10,000
System 2c Warri-Kaduna Pipeline rupture at Abudu	Edo	1982	18,000
Sohika oil spill	Rivers	1983	10,000
Idoho oil spill	Akwa-Ibom	1983	40,000
Jones creek oil spill	Delta	1998	21,000
Jesse oil spill	Delta	1998	10,000
Etiama oil spill	Bayelsa	2000	11,000
Ughelli oil spill	Delta	2005	10,000

Source: UNDP, 2006, P: 184

Large areas of the mangrove ecosystem have been destroyed, undermining its economic value, just as gas flares have impoverished the vegetation (Osuji &Ukale 2000). Oil spills have also necessitated the complete resettlement of some communities, with the loss of agricultural land often translating into a loss of livelihood for farmers, while the psychological and social problems associated with displacements include loss of ancestral homes, familiar surroundings, religious and other cultural artefacts.

The impact of oil spills has been extensive habitat despoliation, enormous financial loss, and poverty leading to the continuous struggles and crises in the Niger Delta Area of Nigeria that later culminated in the kidnapping of oil workers, politicians, wealthy peoples, and even children. Oil spillage occurs through leaking pipelines and storage tankers due to lack of regular maintenance. Some of these facilities have been in use for decades without replacement; 50 per cent of oil spills are due to corrosion. Sabotage and piracy account for 28 per cent of oil spills, with 21 per cent, of the spilt oil being due to inadequate or non-functional production equipment. The main sources of oil spills in the Niger Delta are: aging pipelines; oil blow-outs from the flow stations; oil pipeline vandalism by the local inhabitants; leakages, both accidental and deliberate, from oil tankers on the high seas, and the disposal of used oil into the drains by roadside mechanics.

In another vein, petroleum has also negatively impacted on the environment through oil spillage resulting from activities in the petroleum industry, which include exploration and exploitation, production, processing (tank farms, gas flaring) tank loading, storage depots, transportation pipelining and refinery. Marine biota, especially the young ones, are more susceptible to petroleum pollution: these organisms may not have a chance to recover. It has been asserted that all the various activities connected with oil industries are sources of emission of pollution, and are therefore causes of deterioration of land and water quality in the Delta in particular. Heavy crude may sink and form a blanket on the oxygen needed for respiration and photosynthesis which are themselves needed for plant growth, thus suffocating the animals as well as increasing the river and seabed temperatures which in turn becomes unbearable for both plants and animals, planktons, larvae and small marine organisms. Marine animals in some cases are affected the same way as some sea birds by freshly split oil. Smaller organisms may be easily caught up in large masses of oil, while sedentary animals and plants can do little to survive bantering by heavy stranding oil. Oil spillages (reported or unreported) have caused massive destruction to farmlands, sources of drinking water, mangrove forests and fishing grounds, and decimation of fish, crabs, mollusc, periwinkles and birds. Many of these occurred in the course of production mainly through careless channelling or malfunctioning of equipment (Adeyemi 2004).

Acid Rain in Nigeria

Acid rain has emerged as another major environmental problem in the Niger Delta. There is a series of widespread allegations that gas flaring in the Niger Delta region of Nigeria is contributing greatly to temperature increase and acid rain in this region (Shell Petroleum Development Company, SPDC 1995; Efe, 2003). The consequences of this, according to the host communities, are not only limited to the corrosion of metals, but also lower the quality of rainwater harvesting, acidify other water sources, and deplete soil fertility, leading to the extinction of vegetation species in the area (Akporido et al. 2000; Okecha 2000).

The Shell Petroleum Development Company (1995) asserted that although the occurrence of acid rain is restricted to the foci or vicinity of the gas flares, there is no evidence that gas flaring is the major factor. However, Alakpodia (2000); Okecha (2000) suggested that gas flaring is the major cause of acid rain in the Niger Delta region of Nigeria, and called for more studies to regularly assess the issue of acid rain and its causes in this region. More recently, the occurrence of acid rain has also been confirmed in 18 rural coastal communities of Delta State (Efe, 2006). A mean pH value of 6.4 was observed in the open atmosphere, whereas lower pH values of 5.0–5.3 were seen in the roof catchments of buildings in some coastal communities of Delta State, which was attributed to the proximity of these buildings to gas flare sites and the nature of the roofing materials (Efe, 2006). Acidification of surface and ground water by acid rain in the Western Niger Delta has also been reported (Olobaniyi & Owoyemi, 2004; Omo-Irabor et al., 2008; Efe, 2010b). In addition to the impact on rain pH, it has been suggested that routine flaring in the Niger Delta is linked to thermal pollution, climatic anomalies, extinction of vegetation and animal species and an increase in roof leakages due to a poorer quality of rain (Alakpodia, 2000; Efe, 2002; Onianwa et al., 2002).

Efe (2010b), in his study of the spatial variation in acid and some heavy metal composition of rainwater harvesting in the Niger Delta opined that there is widespread occurrence of acid rain in the area. This varied significantly in space and has strong environmental implications for terrestrial aquatic lives as well as soil components. It was observed from the inhabitants while gathering data that acid rain in the area has precipitated chlorosis and yellowing of leaves, wilting of the leaf tips, and abscission of leaves; and accelerated senescence was observed, and over 40 per cent of tree and other plant species have been lost for over thirteen years. These effects were most pronounced very close to the gas flaring sites where rain pH was lowest (pH 3.39). In most of the flare sites, deleterious effects of acid rain on plants have been reported (Jacobson, 1984; Neufeld et al, 1985). Acid also damages roots and stems, in addition to plant leaves. Such damage to plants is also an indirect threat to the micro-organisms which decompose them, and subsequently the rest of the ecosystem. Jeffrey et al (1981) found that the application of simulated sulphuric acid to a number of crops resulted in decreased yield and growth and foliar injury. A decrease in the growth and yield of crops like cassava, sweet potatoes, maize, melon plantain, and rubber, amongst others, has also been reported in the area potentially due to such effects from acid rain (Efe, 2010 b). This has invariably affected the socio-economic life of the inhabitants of the oil-producing communities in these agrarian communities. Acid rain has also affected soils by removing essential nutrients, leading to soil infertility in the region; and toxic heavy metals have leached from the soil to surface water.

The quality of other sources of water in the area is also affected by acid rain, as most of the rivers and streams are acidified, and as a result contain a high concentration of anions and cations (Okecha, 2000; Ogunkoya and Efi, 2003; Olobaniyi and Efe, 2007). According to the inhabitants, acidification in the region has also led to productive failure in aquatic life. The eggs of some fish species such as goldfish, salamonide, roach, and tilapia have reportedly been killed by high acidity. In addition, amphibians that spawn in streams in the early wet season have been unable to reproduce. Similarly, reduced Ca and increased Cd and Pb concentration in surface water as a result of acidification, result in deformed bone structures and poor growth in fish (Olobaniye and Efe, 2007; Efe and Mogborukor, 2008). Consequently, birds such as loons and osprey that predominate in the area and feed on fish are no longer found. The cornea and mucous layer of the respiratory tracts are very sensitive to acid rain—acidosis, irritation of eye, conjunctivitis, bronchitis and prolonged coughing, and lung disease have been found in the region (Asonye et al, 2004; Efe and Mogborokor, 2008). Health problems have previously been linked to exposure to airborne acidity (Lippmannm, 1985), and kerato conjunctivitis has been reported in a study among children in oil producing industrial areas of Delta State, Nigeria, where it was attributed to pollution in the area (Asonye et al., 2004).

It also causes food poisoning, as the aqueous ion of heavy metals is highly toxic. The high level of heavy metals in fresh water can accumulate in birds and fish, which are then ingested by humans, leading to further health problems. Buildings and structures in the area, according to the residents, have been discoloured and disfigured. Most landlords in the region claim that they carry out routine repainting of their houses every two years because of discoloration by acid rain. Similarly, because of corrosion of their roofs, many buildings in the area suffer leakages. Recent surveys found that over 40 per cent of houses in the region (especially those at the foci of the flare sites) were leaking, and roof repairs or replacement are carried out every three years (Alakpodia, 2000; Efe, 2005,

2010). But this was not so in the non-oil regions where repairs are only carried out after many years. In addition, most car owners in the region reported that their cars were regularly discoloured, and that they had to carry out re-spraying once every three to four years. The bottom plate and body of the car were also affected by corrosion, leading to rust and annual bodywork on the car (Efe, 2010b).

These environmental consequences suggest that there is a need for legislation to put an immediate end to gas flaring; alternatively, it should be converted to industrial raw material for the production of domestic gases. There should be a reduction of emission of acid gases. Acidified wells, rivers and other water bodies should be treated with lime to restore the pH to a level at which fish and other organisms can survive, and rainwater harvested for domestic uses should be purified. All environmental laws for the protection of the environment should be implemented, mass education for the inhabitants of the area should be available, and periodic environmental impact assessments of the region by both the oil company and the federal government of Nigeria should be carried out. The gas flaring operators should plough back part of their profits for the provision of social amenities in the region, and employment should be given to suitably qualified inhabitants of the host communities.

Development and Planning of the Degraded Rural Environment in Nigeria

The predominant style of development in Nigeria is based on the promotion of industrialization to attain the rapid growth required for the desired well-being of the local population (Edoho and Dibie, 2000). This development strategy was based primarily on the supposition that significant incentives to the industrial sector would bring about a highly dynamic increase in all production activities, which would in turn increase production, economic growth, and development throughout the economy (Ashiomanedu, 2009). With such a modernization, the process was expected to enhance the skills of both labour and management, thereby leading to a favourable climate for inward investments, as well as foreign direct investments (Ashiomanedu, 2009, p. 221). The problems with this growth strategy are reflected in the poor social and economic conditions that prevail in both urban and rural areas. This is because there is no social safety net in place to deal with the vagaries of the market or to cater for the weak and poor, who only exist on the periphery of the market economy. Edoho & Dibie (2000), in their review of environmental policies in Nigeria, noted that Nigeria cannot lay claim to be making good use of her natural resources due to the fact that environmental policies have always been initiated by international development agencies and multilateral organizations. Consequently, the environmental policies fail to take into account the real indigenous social and economic characteristics of the country itself. This has led to confusion, rather than clarity, when discussing environmental policies.

Rural development is an important tool for fighting poverty and achieving economic prosperity at the grassroots level (Nwachukwu & Ezeh, 2007), since it is concerned primarily with the improvement of the standard of living of the low income population living in the rural areas on a self-sustaining basis (Mabogunje, 1980; Lele, 1979). The rural areas of Nigeria are inhabited by the bulk of the nation's population (Olayiwola & Adeleye, 2005). They serve as the base for food production, and are also the major sources of capital formation for the country as they engage in primary activities that form the foundation for economic development (Olatunbosun, 1975). In the Niger Delta region, and in Nigeria as a whole, inadequate and ineffective rural infrastructure is a major characteristic of the rural areas. Madu (2007) characterizes the essence of rural development as the improvement of the spatial and socio-economic environment of rural space, which leads to the enhancement of individuals' ability to care for and sustain their well-being. Rural development relates not only to a sustained increase in the level of production and productivity of all rural dwellers, but a sustained improvement of their well-being, that should manifest in increased per capita income and standard of living. It should also lead to sustained physical, social, and economic improvement of the rural community (Titilola, 2000). Ensuring sustainable management of the natural resource base in order to meet people's basic needs requires two priorities for action. The first is human resource capacity-building, and the second is institutional strengthening and orientation (Munslow & Fitzgerald, 1994). These demand redressing the extreme inequalities experienced by the people of the region through the neglect of basic infrastructure and failure to replicate infrastructures to areas of need. Hence, empowering communities emphasizes the need for communities to be able to mobilize their own resources and command a level of outside support.

The dilemma of development in the rural areas of the oil-producing communities of Nigeria is particularly evident owing largely to years of neglect, extensive physical and environmental degradation, and the near collapse of traditional norms and values; and most of the indigenous people generally perceive the oil companies operating in the area as the source of their woes (Samuel, 2008). Similarly, the employment and livelihood opportunities provided are beyond the capabilities of the most of the inhabitants, because of high levels of illiteracy and low technical and managerial abilities. Ever since the launching of the First National Development Plan (1962-68), the oil industry has been expected to play a major role in the life of the people. The overriding strategy from the First National Development Plan to the Fourth National Development Plan (1981-85) has been to deploy the financial resources realized from crude petroleum for the expansion of the economy in order to lay a solid foundation for self-sustaining growth and development (Angaye, 1986).

The Niger Delta is home to a large number of communities amongst the ethnic minority groups spread over the South-South geopolitical zone, and is home to Nigeria's oil industry. The lands and people of this region have borne the brunt of the environmental and social impact of oil exploration and production activities. In spite of its huge resource endowment and immense potential for economic growth, the region remains in a pathetic state of underdevelopment. The arrival of the oil exploration companies has further exacerbated historical divisions and animosities within the region. In the pre-colonial period, and all through the colonial period, the mainstay of the Niger Delta economy was agriculture and fishing (UNDP, 2006). During this period, production of timber, palm oil and palm kernels took place in much of the Niger Delta; rubber mostly in the current Edo, Delta, and Cross River states; and cocoa in Ondo and Edo states was at a peak and earning considerable income for the region and for Nigeria as a whole. However, since the advent of the oil industry, these local communities have lost statutory control over their resource-rich lands, especially with the promulgation of the Land Use Decree in 1978, which expropriated land from the original owners and conferred ownership on the Federal Government and its agent of the state—the executive governor of each state of the federation. This remains a primary source of tension as it nullifies the rights of indigenous landowners who still lay claim to their communal land (Akinola, 2006). Section 1 of the Land Use Decree states that, "all lands comprised in the territory of each state (except land vested in the federal government or its agencies) are hereby vested in the governor of the state, who would hold such land in trust for the people and administer for the use and common benefit of all Nigerians in accordance with the provisions of the Act" (as reviewed by Akinola, 2006). This has resulted in agitation for greater access to resource control by the Niger Delta communities with the emergence of social movements and militant youth groups, and has gradually escalated from civil protestations to arms struggle with huge and very destructive impacts on oil exploration activities within the region.

In another vein there are the macro-ecological problems caused by, or contributed to, by villages. Current settlement patterns create a host of local ecological problems. Wildlife habitat in villages is scarce; native species are replaced with consumptive exotics; streams are channelled, pipes are buried; wetlands are filled and aquifers depleted. Downstream areas are flooded and polluted by quick runoff from acres of paved surfaces. Each of these local problems reduces the ability of local ecosystems to accomplish their ecological functions. Local ecological systems are rapidly losing their ability to produce clean water, air, and food, and to maintain a rich variety of inhabitants—in short, they are losing the ability to sustain life. Each of these environmental problems is related in some way to our rural spatial structure, the design of villages and to the settlement pattern. Changes in land-use patterns take decades, so if our rural settlements are to be ready for mid 21st-century energy and resource scarcities, and increases in population, structural changes must be initiated almost immediately. Human habitat must be restructured so that we live within the limits imposed by our life-sustaining ecosystems and follow the organizing principles by which life flourishes.

To correct the ecological damage caused by natural and man-made activities in Nigeria, we first have to rethink and shift our perceptions. It is impossible to get us out of the rural ecological crisis with the same kind of thinking that created it. We have to think ecologically. A sustainable rural settlement can be built if we can imbibe the mental model which mirrors the "village as a living system". The central insight of the living village concept is that villages and landscapes are living systems. A village is a human ecosystem set in a landscape. Because living systems have been organized through 4 billion years of evolution, they constitute a design model for what sustains life on our planet. In particular, local ecosystems tell us what works well in our particular part of the planet. So, we can look at living systems to learn how to design buildings, neighbourhoods, villages, cities and regions.

To an ecologist, the order of an ecosystem is made up of two interrelated and inseparable patterns: structure and function. The structural pattern of a living system is the form, composition, distribution, and configuration of its parts—rocks, soil, plants, and animals. Ecological function is the pattern of relationships among these parts, involving the movement and transformation of energy, materials, and information. Form does not simply follow function. Form guides flow, which, in turn, shapes form.

The landscape seen in this way is more than a political boundary, site, or location for buildings and streets. It is a complex of seen and unseen elements and forces, below ground, on the ground, and in the atmosphere. Seen from the perspective of function, ecosystems provide many goods and services required for our basic existence. These have recently come to be called "ecosystem services" (Fritjof, 1996; Gretchen, 1997), and include such functions as pollination, protection from ultraviolet rays, purification of water, oxygen supply, protection from floods, and climate moderation, among others. These ecosystem services are essential to civilization and are increasingly imperilled by large-scale human activities, such as urban sprawl, oil spills, wetland destruction, deforestation and pollution as evident in Nigeria.

Ecosystem services do not just provide our basic needs. The biosphere nurtures our mind and soul, as well as our stomachs and lungs. The village is natural, but it is a nature degraded, restoration of a healthy ecosystem in the village will contribute to the restoration of human health and support the development of our human and cultural potential. In the sustainable village, nature will be experienced positively.

Strategy for Sustainable Development of the Degraded Rural Environment

The most degraded rural environment in Nigeria is found in the Niger Delta. Located in the central part of Southern Nigeria, the Niger Delta is Africa's largest delta, covering some 70,000 square kilometres (World Bank, 1996). About one third of the region is made up of wetlands, and it contains the third largest mangrove forest in the world. It is also home to Nigeria's oil industry. The country is the largest producer of petroleum products in Africa, and among the world's top ten, and almost all its production comes from the Niger Delta. Inhabitants of the region bear the brunt of the environmental impact of oil production and pollution from other human activities which include fishing, agriculture, forest resource exploitation and demographic change.

Concern has been growing over this region, both nationally and internationally. In spite of the Delta's resource endowment and its immense potential for economic growth and sustainable development, it is under increasing threat from rapidly deteriorating physical and social environments which are not being addressed by current policies and behavioural patterns. A study of the region by the World Bank (1995) has warned that "an urgent need exists to implement mechanisms to protect the life and health of the region's inhabitants and its ecological systems from further deterioration".

The ecological approach to environmental management is based on the observation that the structure and processes of ecosystems vary with locations. The pattern of human activities should fit the pattern of underlying landscape characteristics, including the avoidance of natural hazards, the preservation of stored resources for the future, and the suitability for various land uses, such as agriculture, housing or recreation. Moreover, the intensity of human activity on the land should be based on the land's carrying capacity—that is, its ability to maintain the healthy functioning of landscape processes.

Unfortunately, sensitive location of human activities does not inherently protect wildlife habitat, population sustainability, or biodiversity. We have the opportunity during this millennium to halt mass extinction. To do so, we have to make some fairly radical changes in land use and management, using applied landscape ecology. We must not only preserve existing, mostly fragmented, wildlife habitat, but also reconstruct and restore many wild lands and multiple-use habitat areas.

The key to managing the degraded environment's development will lie in distinguishing what nature can do on its own, given the right conditions, from what humans must orchestrate. Our success will depend on our ability to: raise individual and social awareness of our participation in life-processes, receive timely feedback about system behaviours that affect human activities, and increase our understanding of the non-linear and counterintuitive aspects of the behaviour and development of complex systems.

Sustainability could be defined as acting today in a way that does not diminish the quality of life and options for future generations. The development of the degraded Niger Delta environment requires a major restructuring of the social organization of land use. This has profound planning, design and policy implications. The sustainable development of the denuded Niger Delta environment can be achieved via comprehensive plans, new form of development rules, regional coordination, policy incentives, citizen action, energy codes, habitat conservation plans, innovative storm water planning, creek restoration projects, solar access ordinances, amongst others, some of which are highlighted in Table 4-4.

Table 4- 4: Rural Strategies for Ecosystem Services

Ecosystem Service	***Degraded Countryside Strategy***	***Sustainable Countryside Strategy***
Energy production	Centralized production: fossil fuels, nuclear power	Multi-scalar, regionally fitted renewable energy, solar, wind, hydro, biofuels, cogeneration, conservation
Food production	Remote monoculture: industrial farms	Diversified urban, suburban, and regional agriculture: community gardens, productive parks
Air supply	Mechanical systems in buildings, no rural strategy	Wind planning: green corridors, staggered and dispersed buildings, windbreaks
Water supply	Municipal supply pipes and sewers, irrigation, stream channelling and burial	Rainwater catchment onsite and buildings: natural swales and streams; creek restoration
Nutrients/materials supply	Centralized production: grocery, gardening, and construction industries; rational truck distribution	Local production; cascading uses: restaurant to community garden, sewage to fertilizer, neighbourhood compost
Waste removal	Trucks and landfills, incineration, sink disposers, sanitary sewers	Composting, recycling, eco-industrial parks, composting toilets, neighbourhood sewage treatment
Biodiversity	Serious habitat fragmentation from land development	Landscape ecology patterns: corridor, patch, matrix
Water purification	Chemicals, mechanical filters	Greywater filtration/reuse: living filters; soil percolation and recharge; constructed wetlands
Waste processing	Settling ponds, chlorine, chemicals, landfills	Constructed wetlands; composting
Flood mitigation	Downstream export: flood walls, levees, channelling; centralized retention: dams and reservoirs	Locating out of flood zones; green roofs, permeable cover, recharge zones: wetlands, site retention

Drought mitigation	Centralized reservoirs, interbasin pumping, aquifer extraction; watering bans	Conservation; cisterns, site detention, local ponds and lakes; xeriscape, native plants
Erosion control	Physical barriers, seawall, erosion fence	Acceptance of natural changes; planting, ground cover, avoiding erosion zone development
Energy storage	Gas/oil reserves	Matched demand/supply cycles buildings' structure; ice, phase change materials; reservoirs, forests, biofuels.
Soil regeneration	Mechanical systems to remove crude oil and other contaminants	Phytoremediation using local plant specie

Conclusion

The environment of Nigeria is being subjected to the despoliations of environmental degradation such as drought in the north, erosion, flood, acid rain and oil spillage in the south. All in all, the Niger Delta region records the worst form of environmental degradation (oil spillage, acid rain), and this is due to oil exploration and exploitation in this region. Based on the environmental despoliations, the inhabitants of the rural areas of the Niger Delta region are faced with problems arising from health hazards to lack of safe drinking water and arable land. In spite of the oil reserves, the Delta has remained underdeveloped and poor. There is therefore the need for government to device a development plan for managing the resources of these areas in a coordinated manner that will ensure sustainability and less environmental despoliations, apart from promoting economic growth, the central goal should be to safeguard the ecosystem and minimize environmental degradation in Nigeria.

Ecological values, until quite recently, were not considered to be important in Nigeria. Biodiversity, clean water and open spaces, seemed to be in "endless supply" in the rural areas of Nigeria, in the nineteenth and first half of the twentieth centuries. However, especially during the second half of the twentieth century, human activities (construction work, agriculture, oil resource exploitation, industrial production of goods and services, etc) and natural hazards have diminished ecological values to such an extent that they have become inaccessible to society, especially in the rural areas of Nigeria. Today, natural values are rapidly disappearing from the rural environment. This realization paved the way for "eco-development" and other green movements in recent decades. Politicians and policy makers have come to recognize environmental problems and the strong social demand for sustainable solutions. As a result, environmental standards were set, and many programs launched to protect the remaining values and where possible to reverse the damage. Environmentalism, from being a revolutionary idea, has become mainstream policy and natural values are now being recognized as crucial public goods, which should be maintained for the benefit of future generations.

The crisis of climate change led to the advocacy for the Clean Development Mechanism (CDM) provided by the Kyoto Protocol, which aims to fund low emission energy production in developing countries. The almost complete failure of the CDM in Africa has been attributed to the complexity of the project management bureaucracy. This lesson may have been learned in preparation for the new mechanism known as Reducing Emissions from Deforestation and Degradation (REDD). Difficulties in verification of protection of tropical forests are anticipated, and the slogan "getting ready for REDD" is the euphemism for capacity building. The challenge of adaptation to climate change will test the multi-layered nature of capacity building, especially in agriculture. Governments lack capacity to create science-based national food security strategies in Nigeria; NGOs need help in understanding the risks posed by climate change at community level whilst the farmers themselves lack the financial capacity to adapt, for example by investment in new seed varieties.

CHAPTER FIVE

REINVENTING PUBLIC POLICY FOR THE MANAGEMENT OF NIGER DELTA CRISES THROUGH ETHICAL REORIENTATION

A.A AGAGU

Introduction

The series of crises that have engulfed the Niger Delta region have more than anything demonstrated Nigeria's failure in its public housekeeping and the hypocrisy that underlies its public policy. It is extremely difficult to explain why an area with abundant oil wealth that is the mainstay of the Nigerian economy remains underdeveloped and poverty ridden. The appalling situation in the Niger Delta region not only shows the failure of our leaders, but also that of public policy in the region. This failure is predicated on the insincerity of the policy actors. These actors, on the one hand, comprise the political and bureaucratic elites, and on the other hand, the economic elites, who, more often than not behave like economic vampires. Thus, in spite of the various pronouncements of government, the various institutions and policies put in place, as well as the quantum of funds allocated to programmes in the region, the area continues to be underdeveloped. This explains why poverty, squalor, with their attendant consequences continue to define the face and the fate of the area.

The basic problem of this chapter is that public policy in the Niger Delta region has regrettably taken for granted the well-being of the people from the area for too long. Unfortunately, in spite of government pronouncements, public policies in the region will continue to fail as long as we fail to address the ethical basis underlying public policy in the country. This is because policy actors would always render the institutions, rules and regulations ineffective in an attempt to divert the allocated resources into their private coffers. Just as Machiavelli saw good armies as the foundation for any good state, it could equally be argued that the foundation of any good policy is ethical uprightness. Over the years in the country, ethical bankruptcy has rendered public policy ineffective.

This chapter will attempt to answer the following questions. One, what should be the goal of public policy in the Niger Delta region? Two, what are the observable products and aftermath of public policy in the Niger Delta region? Three, why have public policies failed in the region? Four, who is responsible for such failure? Five, what can be done? Furthermore, the following hypotheses are put forward. One, public policies and their actors in the Niger Delta are self-serving. Two, the Nigerian environment policy enhances policy failure. Three, public policies in the Niger Delta are geared towards expropriation and exploitation rather than the development of the area. Four, public policies in the Niger Delta follow a top-down approach rather than a bottom-up one. Five, institutions for public policy-making and implementation are devoid of ethical character. Six, policy success in the Niger Delta region depends on ethical renewal of the policy actors and the system at large.

Conceptual Framework

This section intends to provide a conceptual framework that can help to properly explicate the nature of the underlying factors that determine public policy, including that of the Niger Delta of Nigeria. Essentially, the political economy provides an appropriate conceptual and methodological basis for analysis. As argued by Beckman (1983:101), attempts to separate the social science disciplines in the analysis of social issues seriously obstruct a thorough understanding of substantive social problems. He suggested "an urgent need to develop theories and method which allow us to treat issues as social wholes". Political economy thus provides the appropriate framework to achieve this. Political economy provides one veritable theoretical prism for x-raying and analyzing public policy in the Niger Delta region. This is particularly so when we consider the various actors, their nature, their motives, their activities, and the impacts and consequences of their activities on the region. As a matter of fact, the political economy perspective not only considers the explicitly stated objectives of a policy or programme, but also equally explores its implicit objectives. The manner of involvement of the Nigerian state and the political and economic actors, as well as the international capitalist in the oil business on the one hand, and the policy process which impoverish the oil communities, on the other hand require the analytical tool of political economy. Thus, the economic motives that determine what goes into policy agenda, what decisions are taken or not taken, and why projects that have no direct impact on the lives of the people get adopted and implemented for them are clearly brought to the open in spite of ideological or ethnic colourations.

Political economy as used here, offers a broader analytical perspective which explores "political preconditions of economic development" on the one hand and "the political consequences of economic development" on the other hand (ibid:103). In addition, it shows the economic and social consequences of political moves and decisions as well as how economic motives determine political actions and non-actions or decisions and non-decisions. Deriving from this is that the economic and social motives of who gets what, when and how become clear. The political economy that drives the management of oil resources in Nigeria has turned oil which should serve as a means of development of the oil communities and the country as a whole to oil curse.

The Nature of the Nigerian State and its Leadership

Central to the relationship between state and public policy in the Niger Delta is the character of the Nigerian state. Basically, it is a neo-colonial state with parasitic ruling elite "whose main source of material wealth and social standing has been the state (IDEA, 2000: 137). Added to this is that the Nigerian state has a "firm grip on virtually every sphere of human endeavour—from production to distribution, education to religion, provision of infrastructures to social services" (*ibid*). It has been argued that "the privatization of the public sphere by the ruling class has elevated corruption to the guiding principle of governance at all levels to the extent that corruption has become a defining character of the state" (ibid).

Aristotle's postulation that the state is the highest level of association for the realizations of individual good continues to rebound. It is not surprising that many modern states have explicitly stated the fundamental objectives of the state policy. Unfortunately, the situation in Nigeria and many African states are disappointingly quite different. Indeed, much has been written about the colonial origin of the Nigerian state and how the colonizing predators through forcible incorporation of colonial Africa into the international capitalist economy denied it and its peoples a free role to play in their socio-economic responsibility in individual, social, national and world affairs. The colonialists did this through forcible usurpation of these roles through colonization (Onimode, 2000: 72-3). Through colonial political structures and socio-economic policies, the emerging Nigerian state was structurally linked with, and made dependent on, the metropolis.

According to Rodney (op cit: 162-3), colonial Africa fell within that part of the international capitalist economy from which surplus was drawn to feed the metropolitan sector. Colonialism was not merely a system of exploitation, but one whose essential purpose was to repatriate profit to the so-called 'mother country'. This includes repatriation of surplus produced by African labour as well as that of its natural resources. Regrettably, but quite predictably, the post-colonial state of Nigeria, which is a creation of imperialism, has followed a developmental strategy dictated by the interest of imperialism and its local allies, not by those of the majority of the indigenous population (Williams, 1980: 23).

The Nigerian power elites, whether as military officers or as civilians, have been very parasitic on the state. Ordinarily, democracy is expected to give a voice to the people and ensure participation, unlike military autocracy. Unfortunately, as Ake (1995:241) rightly argued, Nigeria is a country that democratized without democrats. He described the Nigerian political elite as the type "which is [as] allergic to democracy as it is neurotic in the pursuit of power". He lamented that the democratization of Africa had focused on the power elite, who are the natural enemies of democracy. Politics in Nigeria is nothing short of struggle for spoils rather than development. Okonta (2008:181) expressed this succinctly when he posited that Nigerian state's chronic inability to deliver development and stable democratic order is bound up within the struggle for spoils. According to him:

> Politics, rather than become the instrument through which the interests of the various contending groups are reconciled and conciliated in an ordinary manner, itself becomes a struggle for the control of these spoils, which in turn are deployed to achieve political ends. Everything is pressed into service in this vicious struggle, including the state (ibid).

Nigeria Federalism and Revenue allocation

Part of the problem confronting the Nigerian state is that of its warped federalism. Apart from structural imbalance, the centre is extremely strong. Either by default or design, the centre not only concentrates political power, but also economic power. These powers it uses indiscriminately and selectively to cow or terrorize the constituent states. Lending credence to this is Nwabueze's analysis of how former President Olusegun Obasanjo subverted Nigeria's federal system. He opined that the subversion by President Obasanjo of the federal system established by the Constitution consists in very significant degree of a deliberate policy matched by actions to degrade the status of the states and their governors and to bolster up that of his federal government as the sole repository of the country's sovereignty. As far as President Obasanjo is concerned, the state governors are only his agents, and subject to his direction (Nwabueze, 2007 xxvi-xxvii).

The Nigerian state is a form of Leviathan that subjugates its constituent units, either as states or communities. Okonta (op cit: 215) linked this with the crisis of democracy in Africa. He opined that "the crisis of democracy in Africa might be attributed to a flawed nation-state project where the ways in which power is exercised and contested by communities". According to him, "as the Ogoni Bill of Rights makes clear, the Ogoni view the Nigeria state as a predatory institution, an incomprehensible Leviathan whose forms of rule run against their own conceptions of authority and the norms and values that legitimize it" (ibid). These inadequacies portend serious threat to the polity and public policy as there is in-built level of suspicion.

The nature of the Nigerian state and its leaders determine the nature of the country's federalism. Unfortunately, as argued by Ihonvbere (2003: 187), most discussions on political restructuring in the country have been isolated from a serious and holistic attention to the character of the Nigerian state. Ihonvbere argued further that

> The state has never been able to build an appreciable degree of confidence among Nigerians, ensure some discipline within the ranks of the elite, manage the economy in the interest of the people, or construct the much needed platforms of inclusion, tolerance, and participation. As well, the state has been captured and privatized by a tiny fraction of the elite that use public institutions and resources to terrorize non-bourgeois communities, abuse human rights, loot public funds, and mortgage the future of the citizenry.

The unwholesome nature and character of the Nigerian state continues to subsist because of the nature of the Nigerian elite. This is why Ihonvbere posited that "the character, organization, discipline, world view and politics of the Nigerian political elite negate possibilities for democracy and federalism" (*ibid*: 193). The unending dispute for revenue allocation and the recent clamour for resource control are part of the products of the crisis of the Nigerian state and our peculiar federalism.

Assessment of Government Policies on Niger Delta

Two sets of evaluation criteria will be adopted in the assessment of government policies in the Niger Delta region. The first is to employ the explicitly stated objectives of each of these policies in the assessment. The second is to identify the implicit motives of the policy makers. This is particularly imperative because it is this that guides the motives of policy actors and the direction of policies in this region. An examination of the explicit objectives of Niger Delta Development Board (NDDB), the Oil Mineral Producing Areas Development Commission (OMPADEC), as well as the Niger Delta Development Commission (NDDC) shows that they were all designed to achieve both physical and human development in the area as well as to redress the environmental degradation in the region. In reality, each of these bodies has fallen seriously short of expectation. For instance, in the case of OMPADEC there was more of an emphasis and commitment to the award of contracts than any evidence of actually functioning projects. Moreover, the body was highly centralized and foisted on the commission an upward-downward approach to management. Furthermore, OMPADEC was also criticized for the indiscriminate award of contracts, over-pricing, policy drift, and ineffectiveness among others (Roberts, 1998:33-34).

With respect to NDDC, it has a broader mandate than the OMPADEC. The NDDC, in formulating and developing the area, is expected to come up with the master plan of the area to enhance sustainable development. It is almost a decade since the establishment of the NDDC. Yet it still has serious challenges in ameliorating the plight of the people from the area. In spite of the fanfare with which the NDDC was established, it has not been able to solve the multiple problems confronting the region and its people. The rise in the spate of youth restiveness and militancy with the attendant kidnapping and hostage taking is concrete evidence that we still need to go a long way to ensure sustainable development.

It is this that makes it expedient to go beyond the explicit objectives and employ implicit or unstated objectives in assessing public policies in the area. This involves bringing to the fore the hidden agenda of the policy actors comprising the political and bureaucratic elites as well as other interested parties. The alliance or the connivance of these various policy actors against the will of the people has been engendered by the nature of the Nigerian state.

Coming to our earlier questions, first, what should be the goal of public policy in the Niger Delta region? Quite relevant here is the suggestion that an oil policy should be formulated with its thrust on the well-being of the people, the community, and sustainability of the environment of the host oil-bearing area in particular, and Nigeria generally. Such policies should be based on a bottom-up approach to planning. It should also be comprehensive in design while taking care of the entire socio-cultural milieu. Even in spite of the pseudo-federalism we operate, any public policy in the area should first ensure the overall well-being of the people and the area as well as sustainable development. This cannot be done through haphazard policies, because "sustainability requires thinking long term, but acting now" (World Development Report, 2003:183). Policies should be stated in clear-cut objectives, and measurable terms with concrete programmes. It is expected that public policy in the region should provide the basic needs for the people, provide infrastructure, alleviate poverty, mitigate the effects of oil exploitation in terms of opportunity cost, land and occupation foregone and environmental degradation in the area, among others.

The second question raised in the preliminary is what are the observable products and aftermath of public policy in the Niger Delta region? Observable facts show that there is apparent neglect of the area in terms of infrastructure and social amenities. At the same time, the welfare of the people has been neglected. The exploitation of oil in the area poses peculiar problems to the people in the sense that their means of livelihood has been eliminated. While the hitherto arable land has been polluted, marine life in the area has also been destroyed. Thus, there must be concrete substitutes to mitigate for all these. It goes beyond providing jobs not only for school leavers, but also for all age grades.

The third question is why *have* public policies failed in the region? It is obvious that these policies fail because of the way and manner they were formulated and implemented. This also includes the conception, the design, as well as the motives of the formulators and implementers. Apart from these, both the institutions for policy-making and implementation have been distorted and have become self-serving. Moreover, the policy environment enhances policy failure.

This fourth question is closely tied to the third. That is, who is responsible for such failure? Many actors are responsible for these failures. They go beyond the political and bureaucratic office holders to include the multinational corporations, some traditional rulers, opinion leaders, as well as some unsuspecting citizens. The fifth question is what can be done? This question will be answered in the second to the last section. Suffice it to state here that there is a need for change of attitude on the part of all and sundry.

The Ethical Foundation of the Niger Delta Crises and their Aftermath

It could be argued that the current crisis in the Niger Delta has an ethical foundation rather than mere administrative ineptitude. These ethical issues include the perverted notion of the elite about the importance of the region on the one hand, and the prevalence of corruption, injustice, and lack of respect for human dignity on the other. The perverted notion of our elite explains why public policy actors in the country had for so long failed to recognize the importance of the Niger Delta region to the country. This disgusting situation has been aptly expressed by Roberts (2004:85) when he noted that "from the determination of policy to the production and consumption of products, the sector is characterised by ubiquitous inequalities in the distribution of values. He argued that:

> Most paradoxically, communities in the oil activity areas figure perhaps as the most disadvantaged group for, for while not benefiting commensurately as producers of Nigeria's most important source of development revenue earning for now, they bear the direct and indirect costs of oil production in the country. The correlation of neglect and marginalisation with the distribution of power defines Nigeria as a federation lacking in social justice and therefore fatally threatened both in its development endeavour and … its survival as a nation state (ibid: 85-86).

This has serious implications for the philosophy of public policies in the area. The Nigerian state and its ruling elite were content as long as the region could provide resources to service other parts of the country, as well as provide an avenue for putting up fictitious projects that could enhance their expropriation tendencies. It did not matter what became of the region and its people as long as it could perform those roles. Perhaps such notions derived from the original purpose of the colonial state to exploit its territory unabated. It has thus been possible for the elite to take the people for granted for too long. This notion defies normal logic, that the area that lays the proverbial golden eggs should rather be treasured. It is in the light of this that Campbell (2010:64) posited that "oil is the glue that holds Nigeria together. It motivates the *ogas* to preserve the federation and generates most government revenue and nearly all of Nigeria's foreign exchange".

Furthermore, the cancerous nature of corruption has depleted the possible gains of the little resources that have been deployed to the area. Unfortunately, this has produced some unexpected consequences,. which have grave political, social, economic, human and other related costs.

According to Bertucci (2003), "the long-term costs of violent conflict are incalculable, not only in terms of physical destruction and human suffering, but also because it creates fierce and implacable enmity between communities and shatters a nation's vision, trust and allegiance."

Re-inventing Public Policy in the Niger Delta Region through Ethical Re-orientation

Naturally, there are imperfections in individuals and society. Even the supposedly perfect constitutions have their imperfections. This explains why specialized bodies such as the judiciary have to be saddled with the responsibility of interpreting it. Usually, it has become a norm to stipulate minimum acceptable standards guiding the conduct of public office holders. Thus, a corpus of knowledge has emanated on what constitutes the type, scale and quality of ethical standards that should guide the formulation as well as implementation of public policies (Sani, 2008:63). Hence the various principles and theories on the level of morality, the code of conduct and the general ethical standards with which public office holders should uphold and comply *(ibid)*. Critical to this is the issue of transparency and accountability. Moreover, no individual—no matter his or her status—should operate outside these norms. Neither should any institution be exempted. The availability of effective sanctions for defaulters often sustains such norms. In many countries this has enhanced effective public housekeeping. However, where there is disregard for these norms, there is usually ethical crisis.

Ethical crisis pervades Nigerian public life. It manifests among the political leaders, bureaucrats, the general citizenry, and even among religious leaders and traditional leaders. Ethical problems among Nigerian political leaders manifest in many ways. They include reckless pursuit of power, electoral fraud, abuse of power, nepotism, corruption and embezzlement, among others. An ethical crisis creates grave problems for development in the country. Indeed, it under-develops the country and the citizens. The problem of development in Nigeria is not a result of lack of competent personnel or absence of adequate financial resources. Rather, it is more associated with lack of discipline and the prevalence of the various ethical lapses. This explains why Abdullahi (1986:9) argued that the problems of development are not necessarily due to the scarcity of the natural factors of production which are required to bring about development, but rather an unending struggle among Nigerians to gain advantages over fellow Nigerians. He described corruption as one of the greatest obstacles to national development.

There is no gainsaying that public policies in the Niger Delta region over the years have failed to achieve the expected goals. By this we mean the expectations of the people and the international community. Furthermore, governments have realized this over the years and have made several attempts to improve on them. Sometimes, institutions and organizations have been redesigned, changed, or reinforced. However, most of the efforts have not met the desire expectations. Here, we shall attempt to answer the fifth question about what can be done.

In a political setting where public policy has failed, it is quite expedient to actually re-invent it. Re-inventing public policy requires not only using public policy to meet the basic needs but also ensuring sustainability. The issues that are necessary in the attempt to re-invent public policy in the Niger Delta would depend on the core causes of the observed failure. One central foundation we have identified is ethical crises among the policy actors and policy network. Hence, the main thing this chapter tends to emphasize is ethical re-orientation. This requires everybody in the policy network to be ethically sane. It is this that makes everybody his brother's keeper. It makes everybody public spirited and work in the public interest. Considering the hypotheses put forward in the introduction, a common denominator of ethical failure can be found among the six. In the first hypothesis, because public policies and their actors in the Niger Delta are self-serving, the various policies put forward by government always fail. It is this single factor that also affects all other hypotheses.

One, public policies and their actors in the Niger Delta are self-serving. These actors include individuals, institutions and organizations like multinational oil companies. Public policy, which is a general plan of action adopted by government to solve problems, exhibits a different character in Nigeria. A survey of the various aspects of Nigeria's public life since independence portends a state of pathology. The reality is that our public policies are half-baked and poorly thought out (Ihonvbere, 2004). Understanding the policy actors requires taking into consideration their purposes, ideologies, motives, interests, and attachment. Thus, both the political and bureaucratic office holders as well as those carrying out business in the areas and the contractors to a great extent are self-serving. In other words, their roles in public policy process are governed by what would accrue to them and their clientele.

Two, the Nigerian policy environment enhances policy failure. Ecology of policy impinges seriously on its outputs. Hence, there is the need to ensure a more favourable policy environment. Nigeria suffers from most problems confronting many third world countries. These problems range from policy imposition, hasty adoption of imported policies, lack of policy goals, lack of social acceptability, lack of continuity in commitment to policy, lack of clear definition of responsibility and co-ordination, as well as compromises during implementation. Others include lack of political will as well as lack of confidence by the citizenry (Egonmwan, 1991:242-251).

Generally, Nigeria's policy environment can be adequately captured from four perspectives: the perspective of policy formulation and adoption; the perspective of policy implementation; the perspective of the country's socio-political milieu; and the obtrusive international environment governed by international political economy. In the main, Nigeria's policy environment is characterized by the following. The first is importation of policies. This denies the citizenry of the necessary participation expected of them. Inability to accommodate inputs of the citizenry robs most policies of their expected richness and necessary support from the people. In order words, policies are made for the people and not with the people.

Second, and emanating from above, is the unnecessary haste in the adoption of policy. It is as if government alone knows everything about the people and the society. From these two features, policies become nothing short of imposition. Policy-making becomes devoid of policy analysis as well as implementation analysis. It is therefore not surprising that many of our policies end up in confusion and failure.

Third, policy implementation is often subjected to the whims and caprices of the chief executive, or his associates. This means there is no commitment to policy continuity or stability. This is because policies are not tied to national goals. Deriving from the above is the culture of constantly abandoning policies initiated by previous governments.

Fourth, policy implementation is often affected by erratic budgetary allocations. Usually, this is governed by the fluctuating price of oil at an international level, as well as government's priority in terms of policies and programs.

Fifth is the late release of funds for programmes even when funds are available. One uncharitable development in the country since 1999 is the late passage of the federal budget. This greatly affects policy implementation. For instance, the NDDC budget for the year 2011 was approved only in 2012.

The third hypothesis is that public policies in the Niger Delta are geared towards expropriation and exploitation rather than the development of the area. The choice of the various revenue allocation formulæ, the determination of the type of federation, the citing of projects, and reliefs granted or not granted are located within the Lasswellian notion of "who gets what, when and how?" and the Eastonian notion of "authoritative allocation of values in the society" (Agagu, 2008). If public policies, programmes and projects to redress the injustice in the area in the last five decades could only produce poverty and squalor, then it only demonstrates how the relatively huge funds expended there were diverted to private coffers. Public policy must shift from expropriation to service. It is not enough to say that some huge sum of money has been spent on a project without the commensurate result.

The fourth hypothesis is that public policies in the Niger Delta follow a top-down approach rather than a bottom-up approach. This only shows policy imposition which alienates the people from such policies.

The fifth hypothesis is that institutions for public policy-making and implementation are devoid of ethical standard. Our public institutions have been so over-manipulated that they no longer serve the interests of the public, but only those of the operators and their retinues.

Finally, it is hypothesized that policy success in the Niger Delta region depends on ethical renewal of the policy actors and society at large. What makes the difference between Nigeria's oil communities and those of other countries of the world is the concern and commitment in those places. The position here is that getting out of development crises in Nigeria in general, and the Niger Delta in particular, requires a sound ethical foundation.

For the Niger Delta to occupy its pride of place in the country, and for the people of the area to have a sense of belonging and have faith in the Nigerian state, there is the need for self-examination by our leaders. However, since many of them are actually benefiting from this negative trend, they may even want to frustrate any positive change. Therefore, civil society organizations, the mass media and the public-spirited individuals in the country have to selflessly take up this challenge. The Niger Delta is supposed to be highly developed, and its citizens are expected to be enjoying high standards of living, given the area's resources. However, the nature of the Nigerian state has created grave ethical lapses and situations where nothing works well. There is indiscipline on the part of leaders and followers alike. The resources of the Niger Delta area and of the nation are being depleted as public officers fill their pockets with public funds. The various mechanisms adopted by successive leaders have failed to achieve results because the Nigerian state, its leaders and citizenry are ethically bankrupt—the ones who want to be honest and transparent are often frustrated. As long as the Nigerian state and the various actors that determine the ebb and flow of government are morally bankrupt, development will continue to elude the region, the country and—by extension—the Nigerian citizenship would be problematic. There is therefore the need to redefine the purpose and nature of the Nigerian state. In addition, there is the need for well-meaning Nigerians championing enduring reform in the country to begin to focus on and mobilize civil society towards a new ethical agenda. The current trend whereby society is tolerant of, and encourages corruption must give way to one in which society really serves as the custodian of national ethics and can sanction leaders and followers alike. This, I believe, will be the only path to the development in the Niger Delta as well as the nation at large. It will of necessity, bring about harmony between the citizens of the region and the Nigerian state. It will produce a country where public ethics would engender genuine development and general well-being.

It is obvious that the current nature of the Nigerian state cannot engender development or any meaningful reforms in any sector. While the nature of the Nigerian state continues to rob it of people orientated development, it is being accentuated by the type of elite foisted on the country. There is therefore the need for a new conception of such a state that would be development orientated and that can nurture elites who can accomplish this (Agagu, 2007).

Managing the current systems better would not yield much difference—we must seek to transform it. In recreating the Nigerian state, four issues are quite germane. One, there is the need to redesign a state that is based on obligation between it and the citizens. This will create a state which will not only protect the people but also serve them in its totality and ensure that they enjoy the good life. Such a state should be development orientated. The configuration of the state, as well as the locus, focus and deployment of power, must go all out to accomplish this all important purpose of serving the citizens. Two, there is the need for the emergence of selfless, non-imposing, and democratic orientated elite "with a holistic world view who would always appreciate the value of dialogue, negotiation, and compromise in the interest of larger national project" (Ihonvbere, 2003: 209). The defining character of such an elite is that its interest is subjected to that of the state, rather than that of the state being subjected to its own interest. The elite today "is still factionalized and fractionalized. Its national projects is still heavily mediated by primordial considerations, loose alliances, political irresponsibility, and a seemingly pathological fixation on primitive accumulation… its commitment to a national project is shallow" (*ibid*).

Three, all interest groups, ethnic groups, religions groups, political parties, labour unions, student unions, etc., must submit their various interests to that of the state. All religions and ethnic groups in the country have very sound and dependable ethical foundations, if we are to be sincere with one another. They must use their strength in their diversity to foster a new state that must serve the interest of the corporate state and the citizens.

Four, policies, development and reforms must now be redefined in which the citizens and the interest of the overall state are the focus. This is guided by ethical reorientation. There is a need to build harmony between the state and the citizens on the one hand, and the elite and the masses on the other. Any reforms embarked upon by the current crop of that elite can at best be superficial. Under the present condition "the character of the state and its custodians remain an obstacle to very much needed national dialogues much less negotiations for reforms" (Ihonvbere, 2003:210).

The process of achieving this new state formation, and the new Nigerian personality for the elite, and the citizenry alike, must be based on what could be referred to as a "new deal". It must be based on an open, transparent, inclusive participatory dialogue or process of constitutional amendment. The example from South Africa shows that with determination and commitment, it is quite possible to recreate a new state that would serve the people and be development-driven. The fact that the oppressive, racist and apartheid state of South Africa, with a racist ruling elite could become an egalitarian state with egalitarian ruling elite shows that similar change is possible in Nigeria (Agagu, 2007). There is the need for a kind of state, a kind of democracy and governance "that upholds the good society" (Shah and Goss, 2007:29).

Concluding Notes

The general failure of public policy in the Niger Delta derives from many factors. These include problems associated with the nature and character of the Nigerian state and its federalism. Others are the nature of the policy actors and the elites as well as that of the public institutions that have been bastardized. Coupled with these is the unfavourable policy environment. In addition, public policies are half-baked and poorly thought out (Ihonvbere, 2004). Yet central to all these is ethical crisis. Thus, to ensure that public policies in the Niger Delta work, the ethical foundation of our society and public housekeeping must be addressed. It would indeed require a form of re-inventing public policy through ethical re-orientation. Achieving this requires serious and persistent advocacy, education and leading by example. Ethical re-orientation is necessary to achieve workable and development orientated policies. Achieving this would equally require a re-created Nigerian state and elites with new vision and morality.

CHAPTER SIX

BUDGET AS A TOOL FOR SOCIAL DEVELOPMENT: A REVIEW OF RIVERS STATE CAPITAL BUDGET (1989-2009)

STEVE O. TAMUNO AND TITUS UDOM

Introduction

A budget is a financial estimate of income and expenditure of an organization for a period of time. All organizations carry out budgeting and budgetary controls to varying degrees of expertise, ranging from individual/families, governments, not-for-profit organizations and private business organizations. Budgeting is key to planning and control. As a planning tool, it gives the direction the organization will go and the resources that will be required/deployed to execute the programmes, projects and activities for the budget period. Also, it enables businesses, governments, private organizations, and households to set priorities and monitor progress towards selected goals. Variances between the estimates (budget) and actual expenditure are compared, explanations provided and corrective measures taken if necessary. Most organzations have short (usually one year), medium and long-term budgets.

Depending on the business of the organization, the budget may be broken down into revenue, operational (recurrent) and capital budgets. Recurrent expenditure is for day-to-day running of the organisation, e.g. staff salaries, rents and stationery, while capital expenditure is for building or acquiring fixed assets that will last or contribute to the productivity of the organisation for more than a year, e.g. buildings or motor vehicles. Private business organizations exist primarily to make a profit (by providing private goods and services paid for by customers), while the public sector is there to provide social services, otherwise called public goods. The need for much of the government expenditure arises from the fact that some goods will not be provided at all by a free market economy (public goods such as roads), and that others will be under-provided (merit goods, e.g. education). In a free market economy, goods and services will only be provided if firms can ensure they will receive payment for them.

A business budget is generally used as a tool to formulate intelligent decisions on the management and growth of a business venture. A government budget, on the other hand, is a plan for the collection and expenditure of monies needed to carry out the social, military, and economic policies of an administration. Government budget and expenditure is a key tool for fiscal policies. In our economy that is dominated by the public sector government expenditure is key to social and economic development.

For federal, state, and local governments in Nigeria, the chief executive officer—for example, the president, governor, or council chairperson—prepares the annual budget on the basis of estimates submitted by departments and agencies. The budget is then presented to the National or State assembly, which may modify the estimates and rearrange priorities. The legislature enacts appropriation bills to provide government agencies with authority to enter into financial obligations. An independent body (the office of the auditor general) performs an audit to see that agency expenditures are consistent with legislative directives. Thus, there are four stages of budgeting: preparation, authorization, execution, and audit.

The cash basis is used in budgeting in the public sector. In other words, any unspent money within the period must be returned to the government treasury, it is not carried forward to the next year. The private sector, on the other hand uses the matching/accrual concept. Here, revenue and costs are matched to the accounting period to which the transaction occurred, whether or not cash was spent.

In the private sector, revenue and costs estimates are driven by the economic forecast and business activities that the enterprise wants to embark on for the period. Government policies also affect private sector investments and budgets. It is worth noting that all costs incurred by business organizations must be recovered (with surplus) from customers if they are to make a profit. The budget preparation, approval, tools, and controls in the private sector are approved by the management of each enterprise.

This chapter is organized into four sections. Section two provides a theoretical framework and background literature of budgets and budgetary allocation in Rivers State. Section three presents the data and discusses the results. The conclusion and recommendation are contained in section four.

Background and Literature Review

Conceptual Clarification

In 1890, Alfred Marshall wrote that "health and strength—physical, mental and moral—are the basis of industrial wealth; while conversely the chief importance of material wealth lies in the fact that when wisely used, it increases the health and strength, physical, mental and moral of the human race". The above aptly underscores the goal of every good government, which is to improve the social welfare of its citizens. Section 14 (b) of the 1999 constitution of the Federal Republic of Nigeria states that "the security and welfare of the people shall be the primary purpose of government".

According to Claude Ake, people at the receiving end of development and their well-being are the supreme law of development. He further opines that "development strategy is always contextualized in a particular state, social structure, culture, and meaning. It implies a structure of politics, but it also influences political interactions, practices, and outcomes" (Ake, 2001) cited in Elumilade etal (2006).

Government expenditure is normally divided into recurrent and capital expenditure. The recurrent is used for day to day running of government institutions, while capital expenditure is for development of social and economic infrastructure and utilities. Capital expenditure is spending on assets. It is the purchase of items that will last and will be used time and time again in the provision of a good or service. In the case of the government, examples would be the building of a new hospital, classroom blocks, the purchase of vehicles, new computer equipment or networks, building new roads, and so on. The breakdown between these two types of spending is very important. Capital expenditure has a lasting impact on the economy and helps provide a more efficient, productive economy. A new hospital, for example, will be much more efficient and allow more patients to be treated for many years into the future. In general, capital budgets in governments have multiple roles: as instruments of fiscal policy and to improve the net worth of government, and—particularly in the area of economic infrastructure—as vehicles for economic development Jacobs (2008).

The United Nations' System of National Accounts (SNA) and the IMF's Government Finance Statistics Manual 2001 (GFSM) prescribe how a government's consumption and investment activities should be separately recorded in the government budget and in accounting records and statistics. Box 6-1 below provides an overview of the possible methods to define "capital."

Box 6-1. Defining Capital

Governments around the world may define "capital" in different ways. *Capital spending is generally about physical assets with a useful life of more than one year.* But it also includes capital improvements or the rehabilitation of physical assets that enhance or extend the useful life of the asset (as distinct from repair or maintenance, which assures that the asset is functional for its planned life). Capital spending is sometimes equated with *investment* or *development spending*, where expenditures have benefits extending years into the future. Under this definition, governments may include physical assets for government use (for example, office buildings), physical assets of a public good nature that also enhance private sector development (for example, roads, water systems), and intangibles (for example education, research). It can be quite difficult to distinguish between investment and non-investment expenditures, and if investment spending receives favoured treatment in the annual budgeting, nearly all spending, whether recurrent or not, will end up being classified as investment. Every government establishes some arbitrary cut-off point to distinguish capital from current expenditures. For budgeting purposes, the relevant distinction is between capital and current (or operating) expenditures. Current expenditures are purchases of assets to be consumed within one year, regardless of expenditure size. Small expenditures (for example, less than US$25,000) are recurrent, regardless of the fact that it could be consumed over a period longer than one year.

Source: International Monetary Fund (IMF), 2001

For many countries, separate current and capital budgets—i.e., a "dual budget" process—have their origins in the public finance management policies and structures established by colonial administrations. These administrations distinguished clearly between the recurring operational costs involved in maintaining a narrow range of government services and the "developmental" expenditures needed from time to time to establish new facilities or new administrative functions (Webber, 2007).

Development assistance donors have reinforced this separation over the years through their traditional preference for funding of "development" activities, while at the same time shying away from the "consumption spending" associated with current expenditures. This traditional view of current expenditures as being of lesser economic importance, or merit, has diminished in recent years, as donor agencies now sponsor social recurrent activities such like HIV/AIDS campaigns, immunization, capacity building and economic empowerment.

Capital budget allocation and drivers

There are several factors the government considers in allocating resources to specific areas or sectors. To a large extent, sectoral allocation should be driven by government policies, goals, socio-economic realities, and macroeconomic and social indices. However, we see in some cases that these social realities are often sacrificed on the altar of political exigencies and the personal aspirations of politicians and government officials. Sturm (2001) and Quijano (2005) cited in Abdullateef et al (2008) categorized government budget determinants into three categories:

1. Structural variables which includes a degree of urbanization and population growth;
2. Economic factors, which include government budget deficits, government debt, interest payment of government, private investment, foreign aid, degree of openness, and foreign direct investment;
3. Politico-institutional factors, which include political ideology, electoral cycles, coalition factors, and political freedom as well as political instability.

According to Washington Trend (2009), state economic, demographic, and social trends are related to one another and, in turn, affect government policies on spending and taxation. A strong economy, for example, attracts more people to the state, which in turn boosts state tax collections. At the same time, however, increases in population also put additional pressure on such areas of state responsibility as public schools, prisons, and social services. Social developments, such as crime rates and the incidence of teenage pregnancies, also contribute to demands on public resources.

Vital statistics are required for effective budgeting so that resources are deployed where they are most needed and the greatest impact will be felt. In all sectors of the economy, key statistics and performance indicators should be available to guide government in budgeting, policy formulation and strategic decision-making.

Capital budgeting decision is one of the decision-making areas of a financial manager that involves the commitment of large funds in long-term projects or activities. Consequently, it affects management decisions about the future that are not certain. The capital investment decision is usually irreversible: once an organization has committed funds to a project, it must see the project through to the end, or else it might lose all the money initially committed (Elumilade et al., 2006).

This means that careful planning must go into the capital budgeting process to ensure government objectives are achieved and the social welfare of the citizens is secured. It is also important that government capital expenditure is well targeted to ensure there is value for money. Across the country, millions of naira have been wasted in white elephant projects, most of which have been abandoned.

The ways government budgets are allocated have an important impact on economic development. This is because meaningful budgetary allocations to sectors of the economy could bring government closer to the people. According Gupta et al. (2001) cited by Abdullateef (2008), budgetary allocations to some key sectors of the economy through its positive effects can enhance equity and reduce poverty. The productivity of these allocations depends on the efficiency of resource allocation within the sectors. Gupta et al. (1997), in a cross-sectional study of 38 African countries, attempted to measure the efficiency of government expenditure and concluded that increasing budgetary allocations for education and health may not be the only or most effective way to increase education and health output, and that more attention should be given to increasing the efficiency of expenditure.

In Rivers State, and in Nigeria as a whole, the issue of corruption is of great concern. Transparency International, a global anti-corruption watchdog, rated Nigeria 130th out of 180 countries surveyed, awarding it 2.5 out of a possible 10 points on its 2009 corruption index. Obviously, corruption impedes development and reduces the efficiency of government expenditure. Though billions of naira are budgeted and spent yearly, there is little on the ground to show for it. The governors of the Niger Delta region have been accused of corruption. In fact, two governors from the region that served during 1999—2007 have been convicted on charges of corruption, and have served various jail terms. Others still have cases in the court with the Economic and Financial Crimes Commission (EFCC), the Nigeria anti-graft watchdog. The Niger Delta Citizens and Budget Platform (NDCBP), while commenting on the Rivers State 2009 budget, observed that Rivers State is ranked as the largest economy in Nigeria after Lagos State, and benefits from the 13 per cent derivation. It unarguably emerges among the highest earners of revenue in Nigeria. However, Rivers State fares poorly in all development indicators even in comparison with other less affluent states in the country. It is prone to internal conflict and militancy, fuelled by a culture of fiat and corruption leading to the creation of vast private estates by former and serving government functionaries, at the expense of the people of the commonwealth of Rivers.

Socio-economic condition of Rivers State

Rivers State, one of Nigeria's 36 States, was created from the then Eastern Region of Nigeria by Decree No. 19 of 1967. Before then, the territory was referred to as Oil Rivers Protectorate, a name derived from its central role in the palm oil trades of the last two centuries. The state is the heart of the hydrocarbon industry, responsible for a huge chunk of the nation's foreign exchange earnings. It accounts for over 48 per cent of crude oil produced on-shore in the country, and 100 per cent of Nigeria's liquefied natural gas exports. The strategic importance of Rivers State in the economic equation of Nigeria earned it the name "Treasure Base of the Nation". Port Harcourt, the state capital, is known all over the world as the Garden City, because of its beautiful layout and decent environment.

The State has a population of about five million people (from the 2006 Nigerian census) from various ethnic nationalities, namely Abua, Andoni, Ekpeye, Engenni, Etche, lbanii, Ikwerre, Kalabari, Ndoni, Okrika, etc., distributed across twenty three Local Government Areas. The State is bounded on the South by the Atlantic Ocean, in the North by Anambra, Imo and Abia States, in the East by Akwa lbom State, and in the West by Bayelsa and Delta States. Rivers State, which is in the Niger Delta, has topography of flat plains with a network of rivers and tributaries. It occupies an area of 10,575 square kilometres. The traditional occupation is agriculture, especially fishing and farming.

There are peculiar challenges of the people by virtue of its geographical location and the oil and gas exploitation that has been going on in the area for the past fifty years. Oil and gas alone have generated 40 per cent of Nigeria's gross domestic product (GDP) over recent decades. Between 2000 and 2004, oil accounted for about 79.5 per cent of total government revenues, and about 97 per cent of foreign exchange revenues. However, the region still remains poor on almost all indices of human development. For most people, progress and hope, much less prosperity, remain out of reach. Instead, misdirected resources, inappropriate policy frameworks and a poor visioning of what development should look like have destabilized their societies, and stoked deep and proliferating concerns (UNDP, 2004). The UNDP Niger Delta human development report, painted a grim (but true) picture of the state of affairs in Niger Delta and by extension Rivers State as follows:

> In reality, the Niger Delta is a region suffering from administrative neglect, crumbling social infrastructure and services, high unemployment, social deprivation, abject poverty, filth and squalor, and endemic conflict. Life expectancy is falling in an age of blockbuster oil prices. Energy

> availability is poor in a region that provides one-fifth of the energy needs of the United States. The delta needs to import fuel despite producing over two million barrels of crude oil per day. There is an almost total lack of roads in a region whose wealth is funding gigantic infrastructural development in other parts of Nigeria and expensive peacekeeping activities in other parts of Africa.

The environmental condition is another great area of concern to the people of Rivers State. The natural terrain and hydrology of the Niger Delta have always caused certain environmental problems, especially flooding, siltation, occlusion, erosion and the shortage of land for development. In addition, the exploration and exploitation of oil and gas in the state have resulted in serious environmental damage and distortion of the eco-system, livelihood and health of the people. Frequent oil spills, either through sabotage by criminal elements or faulty pipelines of the oil companies, are common occurrences in the state. Due to the neglect, poverty, poor governance and all the related issues highlighted above, the state has also been engulfed in communal crises, youth restiveness, militancy and criminality as they jostle for their share and control of the oil wealth.

Rivers State Capital budget classification

In the midst of all these challenges, it is a daunting task to allocate and deploy the limited resources to meet the various needs and yearnings of the people. The peculiar terrain of the region makes it difficult and costly to construct roads, drainages, bridges and other social infrastructure. The bulk of the social infrastructure is provided by the government, though the oil companies, as part of their corporate social responsibility have also intervened.

Capital budget may be classified in different ways according to government objectives, reporting needs, administrative convenience, budgetary control procedures or statutory/legislative requirements. The Rivers state capital expenditure is normally broken down into four categories:

1. **The Economic Sector:**
   This includes agriculture, livestock and veterinary services, forestry, fisheries, industry, power, commerce, co-operative, finance and tourism, transport, mining and communication.
2. **The Social Sector:**
   This includes education, health, information/culture, and social development. In recent years items such as women's affairs, youth,

employment and empowerment, local government chieftaincy and community development have been added.

3. **The Environmental Sector:**
   Expenditure on water, sewage and drainage, housing, town and country planning and survey/mapping are categorised under environmental.
4. **General Administration**
   These are miscellaneous capital projects. The 2009 Appropriation Bill included such items as State House capital projects, Port Harcourt ring roads, a football academy, a new teaching hospital, the Greater Port Harcourt city project, the Rivers state reserve and stabilization funds.

To achieve the millennium development goals (MDGs), adequate funding for the social sector is imperative. The eight MDGs are: eradicating extreme hunger and poverty; achieving universal primary education; promoting gender equality and empowering women; reducing child mortality; improving maternal health; combating HIV/AIDS, malaria and other diseases; ensuring environmental sustainability; and developing a global partnership for development. The United Nations and other national and international agencies have adopted minimum budget allocation to the social sector. The minimum allocation is expressed in terms of percentage of total budget or national GDP.

Data Analysis and Presentation

Data analysis strategy

The review of the Capital budget will centre on the four sectors, namely social (mainly health and education), economic, environmental and general administration. The analysis will be done using the real/nominal and the per capita values of the capital budget. The nominal values of the budget have been discounted in real terms using the composite consumer price index (published by the Federal Bureau of Statistics) and the 1985 CPI base index of 100. Discounting for inflation, we are able to see the real allocation to each sector and compare it with the total capital allocation.

In carrying out the per capita analysis, we bring in the element of population. Ordinarily, the population and its demographic dynamics and the socio-economic needs of the people should determine the allocation to each sector. The total population growth is a reasonable indicator of demand for state government services. Growth of select population groups may further drive up demand for specific services like higher education, primary health care or prisons. According to official census figures published by the National population Commission, the population of present Rivers State was 3,187,864 and 5,185,400 in 1991 and 2006 respectively. We have assumed a population growth rate of 2.83 per cent (1989-1990), 2.86 per cent (1991-1995), 2.99 per cent (1996-2000) and 3.5 per cent (2001-2009), in line with the Federal Bureau of Statistics estimates. The capital expenditure and population of the 36 states of the Federation and the Federal capital territory were used as benchmark for the national per capita capital expenditure.

Budget figures for 2004 are estimated, as official figures could not be obtained. As we are working with the budgeted data and not actual expenditure, we assume that cases of carried forward capital budget are not significant. That is, where an item is budgeted in one year but included in subsequent year(s) budget because it was not implemented in the previous year(s).

Presentation of Results

(a) General Overview of Capital budget allocation

Table 6-1 below gives an overview of the budget allocation to the four sectors from 1989-2009. From the table, we see a steady growth in nominal capital allocation from N190m in 1989 to N344, 220m in 2009, except for the drop in 1997 and 1999. In real terms, however, the increase there was not impressive until 2000. The capital allocation rose from N2, 358m to N22, 135 (nominal values), and N70m to N616m (real terms) from 1999 to 2000. This increase was sustained until 2009, when it rose to N3, 302m (real terms). The increase is primarily due to the implementation of the 13 per cent derivation enshrined in the 1999 constitution for the oil-producing states.

Table 6- 1: Overview of capital budget from 1989 to 2009 in N, m

	Economic Sector			Social Sector			Environmental Sector			General Administration			Total	
Year	Nominal	Real	% of Total	Nominal	Real	% of Total	Nominal	Real	% of Total	Nominal	Real	% of Total	Nominal	Real
1989	48	18	25%	39	14	21%	25	9	13%	77	28	41%	190	70
1990	55	19	23%	52	18	22%	28	9	12%	102	35	43%	236	81
1991	85	26	29%	62	19	21%	43	13	14%	105	32	36%	295	89
1992	92	19	21%	167	35	38%	75	16	17%	108	23	24%	442	92
1993	235	31	19%	368	49	30%	227	30	18%	403	54	33%	1,234	164
1994*	259	22	17%	405	34	27%	250	33	26%	443	38	30%	1,358	127
1995	443	22	34%	394	19	30%	220	11	17%	250	12	19%	1,307	64
1996	1,230	47	42%	850	32	29%	520	20	18%	300	11	10%	2,900	110
1997	415	14	41%	269	9	27%	147	5	15%	170	6	17%	1,001	35
1998	816	26	26%	1,090	35	35%	350	11	11%	868	28	28%	3,124	99
1999	568	17	24%	696	21	29%	440	13	19%	655	20	28%	2,358	70
2000	7,770	216	35%	1,987	55	9%	5,287	147	24%	7,091	197	32%	22,135	616
2001	16,156	379	50%	2,418	57	7%	3,612	85	11%	10,422	244	32%	32,607	764
2002	16,156	330	50%	2,418	49	7%	3,612	74	11%	10,422	213	32%	32,607	666
2003	24,191	440	51%	6,025	110	13%	3,635	66	8%	13,995	255	29%	47,846	871
2004	17,788	280	37%	7,154	113	15%	6,125	96	13%	17,144	270	36%	48,212	760
2005	32,600	437	45%	11,497	154	16%	5,590	75	8%	23,243	311	32%	72,931	977
2006	41,687	517	33%	18,710	232	15%	10,268	127	8%	54,140	672	43%	124,804	1,549
2007	56,383	664	40%	20,655	243	15%	8,915	105	6%	54,193	638	39%	140,146	1,650
2008	105,661	1,115	34%	49,288	520	16%	17,836	188	6%	139,887	1,476	45%	312,672	3,299
2009	117,988	1,132	34%	72,404	695	21%	22,900	220	7%	130,929	1,256	38%	344,220	3,302

Source: Rivers State Ministry of Finance (2009); Central Bank of Nigeria (2009)

(b) Capital Budget and Population Growth

As earlier stated in the literature, population and its demographic features are taken as key drivers for budget allocation. The population mirrors the demand for social services, while capital budget allocation is the supply. From fig. 6-1 below, the population has witnessed (as expected) a steady growth rate of about 3 per cent annually, whereas the capital budget remained almost constant from 1989 to 1999. The capital budget witnessed a steep growth from 2000 till 2009 when it levelled with population growth in 2008. The growth is due mainly to an increase in revenue allocation to Rivers State as a result of implementation of 13 per cent oil derivation and also an increase in the oil price during the period. The increase also coincides with the advent of the civilian administration from 1999. During this period, the state government has increased capital expenditure in infrastructural development especially in power and road construction. However, it has not been proved whether the monetary expenditure matches with the physical development, and this is outside the scope of this study.

(c) Rivers vs. National Average Capital Expenditure per capita

Though there is no generally accepted per capita capital expenditure for the states in Nigeria, we attempt to benchmark the Rivers state capital budget with the national average. The national average consists of the capital expenditure of the 36 states of the federation and the federal capital territory over the national population for the period under review. From Figure 2, below, we see that the Rivers State per capita was level with the national average from 1989 to 1999. From 2000 it went far above the national average. The national per capita capital budget witnessed some minimal growth moving from N16 in 1999 to 121 in 2009. This was due to increased national revenue, attributable to oil price increases, during the period. The Rivers state per capita capital budget can be said to have had a geometric progression moving from N17 in 1999 to N597 in 2008 (3412 per cent). As stated earlier, we cannot conclude that the physical infrastructural investment has witnessed comparable growth. According to Gupta et al. (2008), increasing government expenditure may not always guarantee the same increase in social outcomes if government expenditure is inefficient.

Figure 6-1: Rivers Capital budget and population

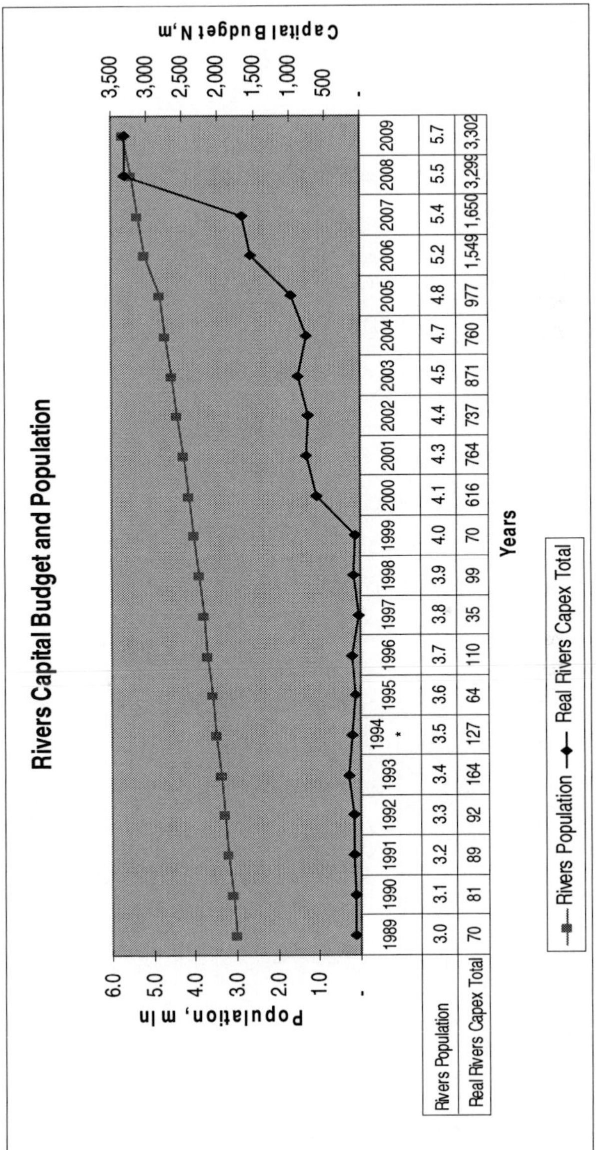

	1989	1990	1991	1992	1993	1994 *	1995	1996	1997	1998	1999	2000	2001	2002	2003	2004	2005	2006	2007	2008	2009
Rivers Population	3.0	3.1	3.2	3.3	3.4	3.5	3.6	3.7	3.8	3.9	4.0	4.1	4.3	4.4	4.5	4.7	4.8	5.2	5.4	5.5	5.7
Real Rivers Capex Total	70	81	89	92	164	127	64	110	35	99	70	616	764	737	871	760	977	1,549	1,650	3,299	3,302

Source: National Population Commission, 2009; Rivers State Ministry of Finance, 2009

Figure 6- 2: Rivers vs. National per capita capital expenditure

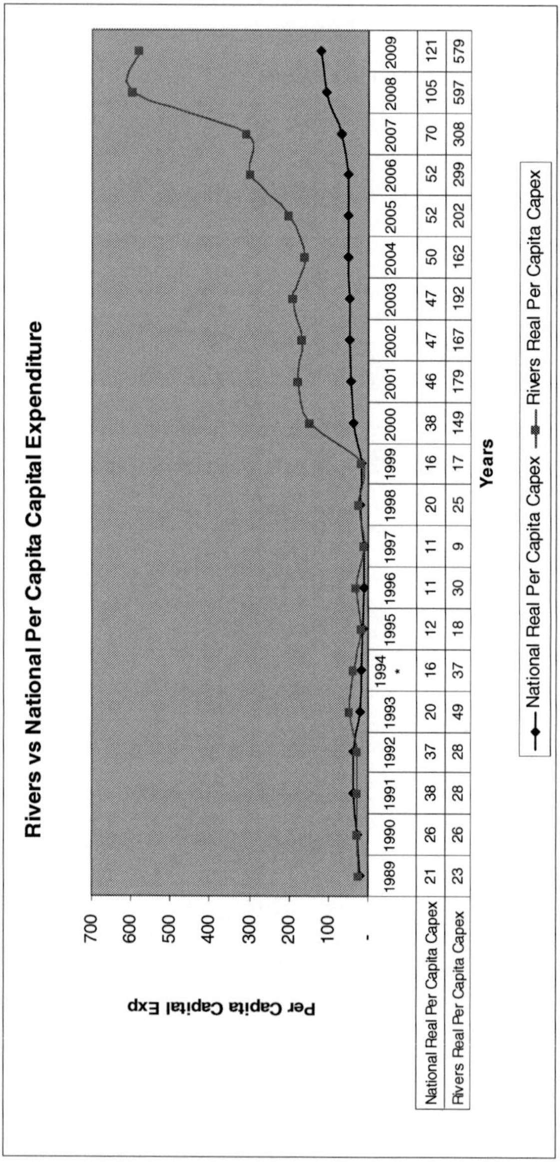

	1989	1990	1991	1992	1993	1994 *	1995	1996	1997	1998	1999	2000	2001	2002	2003	2004	2005	2006	2007	2008	2009
National Real Per Capita Capex	21	26	38	37	20	16	12	11	11	20	16	38	46	47	47	50	52	52	70	105	121
Rivers Real Per Capita Capex	23	26	28	28	49	37	18	30	9	25	17	149	179	167	192	162	202	299	308	597	579

Source: Rivers State ministry of Finance, 2009; Central Bank of Nigeria, 2009; National Population Commission, 2009

d) Sectoral Analysis

We shall now consider the relative capital allocation to the four sectors. How much is allocated to each sector depends on the priority of the government. This priority should normally be determined by the socio-economic necessities and realities of the State. The former governor, Dr Peter Odili, while presenting the 2005 Appropriation Bill to the State house of Assembly, stated that the government shall 'embark on new projects we consider vital to the future prosperity of our state'. Table 6-2 below shows the percentage allocation to the four sectors. From 1989 to 1999 the budget was evenly distributed amongst economic, social and general administration. However from 2000 the budget became heavily skewed in favour of economic and general administration, which jointly controls 75 per cent.

Table 6-2: Average sectoral capital allocation (1989 – 2009)

	Average % Sectoral Allocation	
Sector	1989 - 1999	2000 - 2009
Economic	27%	40%
Social	28%	13%
Environmental	17%	12%
General Admin	28%	35%

Source: Rivers State Ministry of Finance, 2009

Figure 6- 3: Sectoral capital budget allocation

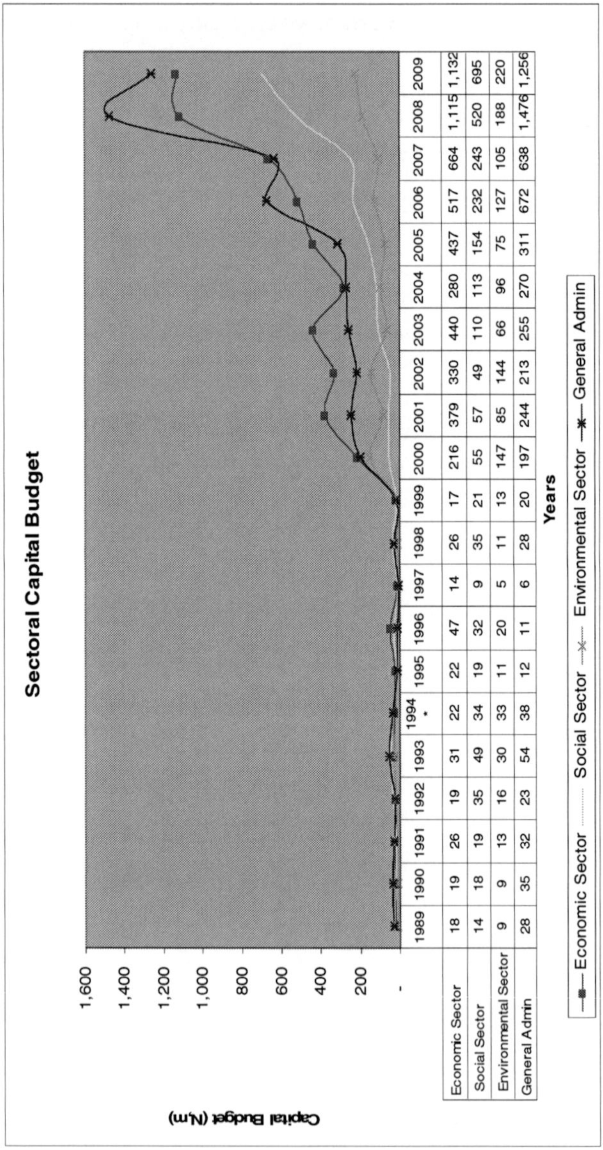

	1989	1990	1991	1992	1993	1994*	1995	1996	1997	1998	1999	2000	2001	2002	2003	2004	2005	2006	2007	2008	2009
Economic Sector	18	19	26	19	31	22	22	47	14	26	17	216	379	330	440	280	437	517	664	1,115	1,132
Social Sector	14	18	19	35	49	34	19	32	9	35	21	55	57	49	110	113	154	232	243	520	695
Environmental Sector	9	9	13	16	30	33	11	20	5	11	13	147	85	144	66	96	75	127	105	188	220
General Admin	28	35	32	23	54	38	12	11	6	28	20	197	244	213	255	270	311	672	638	1,476	1,256

Source: Rivers State Ministry of Finance, 2009

(1) Economic sector:

The economic sector commands a sizeable portion of the capital budget. From 1989 to 2009, a total of N5, 770m was allocated to the economic sector. The two key areas of power and roads/drainages control over 70 per cent of allocation to the economic sector. From 1989 and 1999 the allocation to the economic sector averaged at 27 per cent, but increased to 40 per cent between 2000 and 2009 (50 per cent in 2001 and 51 per cent in 2003). During the last 10 years the State government invested heavily in the power sector though power supply may not have increased proportionately.

(2) Social Sector:

This sector lost its share of capital allocation to the economic and general admin sectors from 2000 to 2009. The average allocation fell from 28 per cent in 1989-1999 to 13 per cent in 2000-2009. The allocation went as low as 7 per cent in 2001 and 2002. However, the sector recovered in 2009 by climbing up to 21 per cent. The social sector—health and education—is the bedrock of any sustainable development. Capital investment in this area includes the construction of classrooms, hospitals, skills acquisition centres etc. From the graph above the social sector is at the bottom (with environmental) of economic and general administration.

(3) Environmental Sector:

Though the total capital budget allocation to the environmental sector has increased over the years, the relative percentage allocation has declined. The average allocation fell from 17 per cent in the period 1989-1999, to 12 per cent in 2000-2009. The allocation has remained fairly stable over the years. The main budget items here are water resources and housing. The poor state or totally non-existent public water supply may not be unconnected with the low budget allocation to this sector. The allocation to this sector fell to its all-time low of 7 per cent in the 2009 budget. The State is faced with numerous environmental challenges which include poor management of industrial and household waste, lack of potable water supply, oil spills and erosion. The low budget allocation to this sector does not show government's commitment to tackle these problems.

(4) General Administration:

There are some items here that may not be strictly classified as capital. For example, the state government security votes in 2006, 2007 and 2008 budgets, and school feeding was part of the general administration capital budget. On the other hand, the general administration also has other items that should rightly be classified into the other three sectors. For example, the 2009 capital budget has items like a football academy, a new teaching hospital, and a new State university that should be classified as social. The general administration has commanded the highest allocation, competing only with the economic sector. The average allocation increased from 28 per cent in 1989-1999 to 35 per cent in the period 2000-2009 (see Table 6-2).

Conclusion and Policy Implications

This chapter has reviewed the capital budget allocation of Rivers State and the sectoral distribution from 1989 to 2009. We discounted the budget in real terms, and included per capita capital budget to analyse the demand and supply of social services using the capital budget. From the study we discovered that the population growth rate was higher than the rate of capital budget allocation in real terms until 2008. The Rivers state capital budget per capita was on a level with the national average from 1989-1999, and went far above the national average from 2000 to 2009. The increase is due mainly to the increased revenue allocation to the State due to 13 per cent oil derivation. This increase also coincides with the advent of the civilian era in 1999. However, it is not clear whether Rivers State has witnessed corresponding improvement in infrastructural and social amenities during this period of increased capital allocation.

The sectoral allocation also followed the 1989-1999 and 2000-2009 dichotomy. The economic, social and general administration capital budget were evenly distributed at about 28 per cent from 1989-1999. However, the social sector lost its share to the economic and general administration sectors from 2000-2009. Most of the capital allocation in the economic and general administration went into power, roads/drainages and security to the neglect of education and health. It is not clear whether the increased capital investment brought corresponding social and economic benefits. The Niger Delta Citizens Budget Platform (NDCBP), in its review of the 2009 Rivers State budget, also concluded that “the sectors (health and education) that bear directly on the development of the state and its workforce are given reduced allocation, while less important ones (like ‘security vote’ and ‘general administration’) get the bulk of the allocation”.

Rivers State has witnessed a lot of youth restiveness since the advent of the civilian administration in 1999. There is a need to increase the capital allocation to the social sector in the area of youth development, education, skills acquisition and employment generation. The population and its demographic indicators should guide the government in its budget allocation to the various sectors, programmes and projects. The government, as part of the budget preparation, should carry out a cost-benefit and social-impact analysis before embarking on any capital project.

CHAPTER SEVEN

MAKING THE COMMONS WORK IN THE RURAL NIGER DELTA: THE ROLE OF WOMEN IN STABILIZING DEVELOPMENT

S. R. AKINOLA, L. ISIDAHOMHEN AND T. A. AKINOLA

Introduction

This chapter uses the Institutional Analysis and Development (IAD) framework to analyze participants' behaviour, pattern of interactions and decision-making in relation to the commons in the Niger Delta. It also analyses the gap created by not involving women in the development process in the region. The commons, according to Oakerson (1992:41), is a natural resource (or a durable facility of human design and construction) that is shared by a community of producers or consumers—forests, minerals, fishing grounds, pastures, parks, groundwater supplies, public highways, etc. The commons can be renewable (grasslands), or not (oil pools). Four sets of attributes or variables are used to describe a commons: (1) the physical attributes of the specific resources or facility and the technology used to appropriate its yield; (2) the decision-making arrangements (organization and rules) that govern relationships among users, as well as relevant others; (3) the mutual choice of strategies and consequent patterns of interaction among decision makers; and (4) outcomes or consequences (V. Ostrom 1974:55; Oakerson 1981:81, 1992:43).

In the Niger Delta, the commons include: renewable and non-renewable resources—(a) oil that produces revenues for the entire nation, (b) forests and (c) water bodies—that all constitute biophysical/material conditions. The participants are: the elite (public officials, scholars) and the non-elite—farmers, fishermen, students, traders, etc. Since women cut across all categories of participants, their role in the development process is critical if development is to be achieved. The present arrangement emphasizes non-renewable resources (oil) at the expense of renewable resources (forests and water bodies). While benefits from oil are skewed against the people, the impact of oil exploration on forests and water bodies is fast eroding the economic base of farmers and fishermen respectively. What a double tragedy for these groups in the commons! The non-renewability of oil requires extra care and a revenue sharing formula that will manage oil in the light of the future. The politics of exclusion being practiced in the region and its consequences of violent reactions of militants, insecurity and reduction in revenues to the federal government confirm that all participants are important in the commons.

The recent amnesty, a form of panacea to redress the neglect in the commons is not backed up by concrete post-amnesty development plans on the part of government. The type and magnitude of guns, grenades and rounds of ammunition surrendered by ex-militants during the amnesty programme reinforces the willingness on the part of freedom fighters to cooperate. However, there is apathy and lack of cooperation on the part of government in terms of preparedness. This has resulted in protests in some cities in oil-producing regions by ex-militants over the non-payment of amnesty allowances (da Costa, 2009). It is instructive at this juncture to point out that any attempt to focus on the ex-militants alone without adequate consideration for women's economic reality, their children's welfare (health, water, nutrition, etc.) and their indispensable role in development will most likely amount to a missed opportunity in the process of finding a lasting solution to the crisis in the commons in the Niger Delta. Moreover, the informal sector in Africa and the world, has greatly accommodated women as they run various developmental projects such as construction of town halls, schools and maternity centres, arranging micro-credits, teaching entrepreneurial/empowerment skills and building self-reliance among counterparts (Olowu et. al. 1991; Sanda, 1991; Awotona and Akinola, 1996; Haglund et. al., 1996; Chazan et. al., 1988; CBN, 2001; Higgs, 2004; and Okotoni and T. Akinola, 2008).

Geographically, the Niger Delta region covers an area of about 110,000 sq. km, about 11 per cent of Nigeria's land mass (FGN, 2008:182). With a population of about 33.5 million, it accounts for about 23 per cent of the total population of the country (FGN, 2008:189). The people live in about 13,400 long-settled aboriginal communities made up of divers ethnic nationalities (Ijaw, Isoko, Ibiobio, Efik, Ogoni, etc.) with over 75 per cent of them lying along the coastal region (Okaba, 2005a,b, in

Okaba, 2008:29). Due to its difficult topography (creeks), about 95 per cent of the people live in small rural settlements of fewer than 5,000. In fact, 85 per cent of this rural population depend on informal enterprises (fishing, canoe carving, subsistence agriculture, blacksmithing, etc.) as their primary sources of livelihood (Okaba, 2008:29).

In spite of the fact that women constitute approximately 50 per cent of the population in every nation (Iheduru, 2002:4), their potential has not been properly recognized or harnessed towards development in Africa. If women constitute about 50 per cent of the population, what role have they been assigned in decision-making and governance? Hawkins (1992:xi) notes that many complex challenges can be ameliorated or solved by empowering those most directly involved with sufficient authority to devise and enforce small scale community solutions. Critical decisions that affect women are made in the Niger Delta without involving this important group. Similarly, a joint Cameroon-Nigeria Committee on Peaceful hand over of Bakassi has no female representation (Tabifor, 2009:5). The same question can be asked about the number of women in the current amnesty committee in the Niger Delta. If women are involved, one can guess the type of issues they will raise—water supply, health conditions, etc. For any peace-making decision to be successful and long-lasting, women have to be actively involved.

In spite of their disadvantaged position, several studies have confirmed the socio-economic contribution of women in various cultural settings (Chandler, 1971; Sanda, 1991; Ahmad and Martha, 1985; Ewusi, 1987; Oppong, 1987; Selolwanne, 1997; Haglund, B. J. A., Petterson B., Finer D. and Tillgren P., 1996; Awotona and Akinola, 1996; and Okotoni and T. Akinola, 2008). Sanda (1991) affirms that women are generally committed to development and transformation strategies. It should be noted that development is essentially a humanizing process that is based on people irrespective of gender status or poverty and oppression levels. To be specific, in 1987, a well-organized and motivated group of village women in Gambia implemented a land reclamation system devised by the government. Consequent upon this, the women in the country were responsible for 90 per cent of rice production and 100 per cent of vegetable gardening (Haglund, et. al., 1996). This experience supports the argument of Elinor Ostrom (1992a) that:

> A successful system exists when those it serves are actually involved in the design, operation and maintenance of their system, this type of self-governing system where section of the society governs itself is essential for sustainable development.

Though the associational life of women in the Niger Delta has impacted positively on their communities, they have not been accorded their rightful position in formal decision-making, where they could demonstrate their full potential towards developmental activities and governance of community affairs. In spite of the fact that the people look forward to seeing development projects completed, deep-seated insincerity, selfishness and deceit on the part of some groups—elites, some traditional leaders, chiefs, political godfathers, some youths, etc.—have dashed the hopes and aspirations of the grassroots. Until the Niger Delta people see oil as a common pool resource, as the people of Alaska did (see Akinola, 2011b) they cannot collectively determine their own destiny, and oil benefits will not trickle down to the grassroots to enhance the citizens' welfare.

This chapter is derived from both theoretical and empirical backgrounds that reflect scholars' and practitioners' experiences on how to make the commons work in the Niger Delta. This chapter analyzes individual and group behaviour in project delivery in the region. Women, as mothers that bear the brunt of the hardship in the villages, are more 'moderate' in their 'reasoning'. They are exempted in matters of plundering and pillage. In order to make the commons work, this paper, therefore, argues for women's involvement in decision making. Applying the Institutional Analysis and Development (IAD) framework, the paper uses data and insider's experience to analyze the missing links in the operations of governments and oil companies in the delivery of socio-economic projects in the region. Specifically, this chapter argues that the perpetuation of the exclusion of women from formal public terrain is consequent upon defective social and political institutions in the Niger Delta. It therefore interrogates the extent to which voices of women are accommodated in both formal and informal decision-making at various levels of government in the Niger Delta. It proceeds with theoretical underpinnings.

Theoretical Underpinning

The theories of collective action suggest that individuals under certain institutional arrangements and shared norms are capable of organizing and sustaining cooperation that advances the common interest of the group to which they belong (E. Ostrom, 1990). This line of thought recognizes that human beings can organize and govern themselves based on appropriate institutional arrangements and mutual agreements in a community of understanding. This is the fundamental argument of the Institutional Analysis and Development (IAD) framework. The IAD believes in an institutional arrangement designed by people who cooperate, based on the rules and constitution of their choice, and are thereby able to resolve socio-economic and political problems which other people (external to their conditions) are not capable of doing for them. Since society is a system of human cooperation, people in any society should collectively relate to and deal with their exogenous variables.

The IAD considers the role of evolution, culture, learning and social norms in the discourse on collective action (E. Ostrom and Walker, 2003). Institutional structures that people have developed over the years avail individuals in the community to make inputs to development in their locality by contributing towards projects (labour, finance and materials) and decision-making in political arenas in rural settings. According to Sawyer (2005:3), institutional analysis helps us to better understand how individuals within communities, organizations and societies craft rules and organize the rule-ordered relationships in which they live their lives. To understand institutions, according to E. Ostrom (2005:3), one needs to know what they are, how and why they are crafted and sustained, and what consequences they generate in diverse settings. Understanding institutions is a process of learning what they do, how and why they work, how to create or modify them, and eventually how to convey that knowledge to others.

The debate on management of natural resources has polarized into private and state ownerships. While private ownership promises efficiency, but often at the cost of community and democratic values, state ownership claims to address these values, but often at the cost of efficiency, as bureaucracy takes its inevitable toll by destroying community and self-governing values. The third sector, which is the self-governing sector, focuses on common-property ownership by voluntary associations of local users. Abundant evidence confirms that local people, through self-governing institutions, can handle complex social and economic issues successfully and equitably sometimes for hundreds of years (Hawkins, 1992:xi).

The commons is like a factory that produces not a series of differentiated products, but a stream or pool of undifferentiated "product" from which individuals take a portion for their use—hence the term "common-pool resource" (CPR), or "the commons". Without coordination, individuals may in the aggregate use too much too quickly, causing the rate of production to fall. Sharing without collective consumption—the commons situation—requires restraint, which in turn depends on coordination among users. Otherwise, individuals continue to consume without regard to the diminishing marginal product of the commons as a whole (Oakerson 1992:42). If a community of users is unable to work through existing arrangements to respond appropriately to changes, destructive competition or conflict may follow. Resource depletion (or degradation of facilities) results—the "tragedy of the commons." In specific cases, the consequences may be soil erosion, overgrazing, impassable roads, diminishing fish harvests, disappearing species, shrinking forests, reduction in quantity of oil, etc.

There is a critical difference between "open-access resources" and "common-property resources", a difference that turns on the very concept of property. Property is a secure claim on a future benefit stream. There is no property in an open access situation, only the opportunity to use something. Irrigation systems are a good example of a common property regime. It has a well-defined group whose membership is restricted; an asset to be managed (the physical distribution system); an annual stream of benefits (agricultural input); and a need for group management of both the capital stock and the annual flow (necessary maintenance of the system and a process of allocating the water among members of the group of irrigators) to ensure continuous flow of benefits to the group (Bromley, 1992:11).

Though theorists decry the "tragedy of the commons", relying on the arid reasoning of the "prisoner's dilemma" to demonstrate the impossibility of long-lasting voluntary cooperation or effective collective action, evidence from contemporary findings suggests the contrary (Hawkins, 1992:xi). The real problem, in many of the cases of the "tragedy of the commons", is the absence of effective group management regimes necessary to allow the sustained use of the resource base over time. That is, an earlier situation of common property has deteriorated into one of open access (Bromley, 1992:12). However, information asymmetry is a major factor that strengthens the "prisoner's dilemma" and the "tragedy of the commons." This the politicians do not recognize in their operations and conducts; only to predicate policy recommendations upon false definition of the problem—the so-called "tragedy of the commons" (Bromley 1992:3). In order to overcome the major weakness of "prisoner's dilemma" and "tragedy of the commons", conscious efforts need to be made to ensure free flow of information—information symmetrical among participants as well as effective management.

From Tunis to Cape Town, from Cape Verde to Comoros, collective action or self-help or voluntary efforts in Africa underlining self-governing values have produced a lasting impact on participants. It has been confirmed that community institutions in Africa possessed self-organizing capabilities through which community members relate with one another in a rule-ordered relationship, sharing ideas, and using their own initiatives and institutional potentials to address problems of daily existence. Examples of local people's provision of public goods using available social capital (associations) are well documented throughout the African continent (Smock, 1971; Olowu, Ayo and Akande, 1991; McGaffey, 1992; Barkan, McNulty and Ayeni, 1991; IDS, 2001; Okotoni and Akinola, 1996; Akinola, 2000; 2003a; 2004; 2005d; 2007a,f, 2008b, 2009a, 2010a and 2011a). Most often, economic aid to developing countries has ignored these small-scale but effective local institutions, mistakenly relying instead on privatization or state ownership to solve development and natural resource problems. Hawkins (1992:xii) shows that even in the developed world, political and economic "progress" too often seems to result in stripping creativity, power and initiative from average citizens. This need not, and should not, happen if leaders can allow citizens or self-governing institutions to operate freely, while government facilitates and monitors to ensure justice and fairness in the operations of these people-centred institutions. If we share with the collective action theories and CPR principles that institutions matter in terms of their influence on cooperation, then the problem of underdevelopment in the rural Niger Delta can be addressed if appropriate institutional arrangements are put in place. If such institutional arrangements can produce four fundamental imperatives of collective action—collegiality, mutual trust, reciprocity and shared community of understanding—then it is possible for the Niger Delta people at community and local levels to cooperate, especially when they perceive that the outcome of the interactions will be beneficial to them all.

Tragedy of the Commons in the Niger Delta

Oil in the Niger Delta was close to being a common-pool resource (CPR) in the 1960s up to the 1980s (three decades). At that time, the Nigerian government exploited it for the development of the country, and the only challenge at that time was that the government did not comply with the rules of the game of CPR by allowing the outcome to benefit the people in oil-producing communities. Even now, oil does not benefit the region where it is exploited. Instead, its exploitation destroys other biophysical entities—forests and water bodies. As expected, the support for food production is eroded by oil spills on forests, water bodies, and gas flaring. The implication of all these is heightened importation and dependency syndrome. Invariably, investment is reduced and the future is bleak for the people.

E. Ostrom (1992b) reminds us that the stock of a CPR may be used jointly, but that the services flowing from that stock are individually consumed. She lists a number of variables that will contribute to the success of a management regime concerned with CPR. Among those variables are: a common understanding of the management problem; a common understanding of the alternatives for operation; a common perception of trust and reciprocity, and a shared perception that decision-making costs less than the benefits from joint action (E. Ostrom, 1992b:301-303). Unfortunately, there is a lack of shared communities of understanding of oil in Nigeria at federal, state and local or community levels. As a result, privileged individuals and groups exploit oil to satisfy their selfish desires while the common man in the Delta wallows in abject poverty.

Though oil is regarded as an asset that belongs to all in Nigeria, the basis for neglecting the source of oil (the Niger Delta) is difficult to establish and justify. This confirms that those that have been running the affairs of the nation do not understand the act of governing the commons. This leadership failure invariably dictates the failure of other sectors and lower level governance units—state and local governments as well as traditional institutions. For example, autocratic tendencies introduced by the colonialists into Nigerian traditional setting produced unfettered traditional rulers and corrupt chiefs in most parts of the country. Our findings in the Niger Delta support these claims.

From the experience of the Assistant Party Manager of Western Geophysical Company (APMEGC) in the Niger Delta (1988-1993) it was discovered that women were completely excluded from governance and their views were not even sought on matters relating to the development of the community. Most of the community development associations have no women executive members. Similarly, youth associations have no female members, and where they do, their views are inconsequential. There is no female member on the council of Chiefs. In the communities, committees set up to oversee development projects are solely made up of men even when negotiations are to be held with either the company or government on community matters— the committee set up to handle this is made up only of men.

This one single reason probably accounts for why most developmental projects in rural communities of the Niger Delta fail. Deep-seated insincerity, selfishness, greed and deceit on the part of some groups—elites, traditional leaders, chiefs, political godfathers and youths, etc.—have contributed in no small way to stunting development and dashing the hopes and aspirations of the grassroots. In every community in which the

APMEGC was involved, it was discovered that women were excited about community development projects and actually looked forward to their early completion, while others were only interested in how they would benefit personally. This is so, because women saw the projects as capable of alleviating their suffering. On the other hand, the culpable among the men folk connived with dubious contractors, company and government officials to either do shoddy jobs or have the projects abandoned completely.

The experience of the APMEGC zeroes in on four development projects in four communities where he was personally involved. For some reason, the names of individuals that were involved in these projects at the community level are coded. Acronyms that start with letter C refer to a chief, while the one that *ends* with C means a community.

1. **Electricity Generator Plant Repair project at KDC[1] in Gokana and Degema Local Government Areas of Rivers State.**
   The Western Geophysical Company (WGC), while operating in the Bonu Prospects, had its base camp in the community of KDC. The APMEGC decided, together with the leaders of the KDC community, to embark on the repair of the community's generating plant for an agreed sum. Some few days later, the chief of the community, Chief CFG, came requesting that half the sum of the project be released to him, and the project abandoned. The chief's demand was turned down. Consequently, the project was not carried out because of the chief's uncooperative attitude.
2. **Electrification Project for BOC Community in Ogu-Bolo Degema Local Government Area of Rivers State.**
   A community-company relations meeting was held on the developmental project between the BOC community and Shell, where it was agreed in 1990 that the community be electrified for a sum of NGN 90,000. The WGC was instructed to handle the project as the field representative of Shell. The APMEGC was assigned to coordinate the project with specific instructions to buy all the materials needed for the project and pay for the transport and

[1] KDC means a community in Gokana/ Degema Local Government Area of Rivers State. BOC means a community in Ogu-Bolo/ Degema Local Government Area of Rivers State.GOC Gokana/ Degema Local Government Area of Rivers State. We do not intend to mention the name of the community because once the name of the community is mentioned people would automatically know the Chief to whom we are referring. This is a sensitive matter, hence the need to code the names of people involved and their communities.

labour. The first shock was that the community representatives did not prepare a list of materials needed, thinking that the money for the project was going to be released to them. All the same, a list was generated which was taken to the market. The materials were bought and transported to the community. However, when the materials got to the community they were shared by the people and the project abandoned. This confirms that the interests of community representatives were not in the project but in the money.

3. **Market Stalls Redevelopment Project in GOC Gokana Degema Local Government Area of Rivers State.**
   After a series of work stoppages occasioned by the activities of Chief CGA and the youths of GOC community in Gokana LGA, a meeting was held between the management of Shell PDC and representatives of the community led by the said Chief CGA. It was agreed that the community market be redeveloped. Immediately after the meeting, Chief CGA who also happened to be the Chairman of the market management committee, demanded to be given the contract to supply the sand for the project. When his demand was turned down, he mobilized the youths again to disrupt the activities of the company until the contract was granted to him, and which he never executed. Also, all the materials bought for the project were hijacked and shared by him along with some few illiterate chiefs. Thus the project was abandoned.
4. **Classroom Block Development Project in Bille, Degema Local Government Area of Rivers State**
   Just as with the GOC community situation, after a series of work stoppages it was agreed in a meeting between the BLC community and the WGC that a four-classroom block be built for the community school, as the old school block was completely dilapidated. Right from the beginning of the project, bickering started amongst the youths on who should supply the sand for the project. After some mediation by the APMEGC the issue was amicably resolved. Shortly after, another problem came up. In an attempt to create employment opportunity for the youths of the community, it was agreed that the labour for the project should be sourced from within the community. This had a very negative effect on the project as the youths employed for the project never wanted to work. All they were after was their wage slip. This action by the boys actually led to the delay in the completion of the

project as the WGC had to leave for another project, which also led to the abandonment of this project.

In all the communities mentioned above, as well as others not stated here, there was not a single woman representative in the course of interaction with the community leaders. It is believed that if women were involved in these project planning, execution and monitoring, the projects would not have been abandoned. The positive experiences in these communities are the fact that the people, especially the women and the aged, are always very happy and enthusiastic about projects that they believe will uplift them. They are friendly and ready to render any assistance. They really look forward to seeing such projects completed. The Negative experiences range from insincerity to deceit, and sometimes violence, because on two occasions the APMEGC and his team were held hostage.

Once there is lack of coordination among participants, individuals exploit the situation to their advantage. Consequently, lack of cooperation among the people of the Niger Delta has deepened the crisis and poverty in the region. The manifestations of the challenges in the region are numerous: (1) immobility, isolation and lack of education; (2) environmental pollution, land dereliction; (3) divide and rule tactics, and exclusive benefits for a few saboteurs; (4) financial misappropriation, corruption and plundering; (5) execution of opposition leaders; (6) military tanks and the annihilation of innocent citizens; (7) seeking peace without justice—the mirage and illusion of the despots, (8) pipeline vandalism, oil spills and oil bunkering by syndicate groups; (9) oil syndicate groups and financiers of political parties; (10) people's agitation and complaints; (11) dashed hopes of the people, etc. For instance, the people walk on pipelines to their farms and fishing grounds, but the same pipelines carry oil worth millions of Naira every day to benefit people outside their (the Niger Delta) locality. What a paradox!

Besides, the rural people, especially women are exposed to various dangers relating to the effect of gas flaring. For example, the percentage of gas flared in the Niger Delta is highest in the world: 76 per cent, followed by Libya, 21 per cent; Saudi Arabia, 20 per cent; Iran, 19 per cent; Algeria, 4 per cent. While, USA, 0.6 per cent, Ex-USSR, 1.5 per cent; Britain, 4.3 per cent. OPEC's total is 18 per cent, while the world total is 4 per cent (Friends of the Earth, 2004, cited in Okaba, 2005a:191). Relying on indications from other data, the cost of living in the Niger Delta is higher than other parts of Nigeria, and so is the depth and severity of poverty. For example, average life expectancy in the Niger Delta is 46.8 years, due mostly to the high mortality rate among young children—of every 1000 newborn, 200 die by the age of 5. This is one of the poorest amongst developing countries (FGN 2008:221), especially when compared with the national infant mortality rate of Nigeria as a whole, which is 14 per 1000 live at birth (Okaba 2005a:55). Access to health was estimated to be available to only 56.5 per cent of the population, and population per one hospital bed was as high as 1,277 people (Okaba 2005a:55). According to Michael Watts (2009:45), there is one doctor for every 150,000 inhabitants of the oil rich states of Bayelsa and Delta.

Educational attainment at primary and secondary levels suffers from a high teacher-pupil ratio—1:42, compared with the national average of 1:36. This high ratio inevitably reduces teachers' ability to impart knowledge (FGN 2008:221). The poor inculcation of knowledge and consequent poor academic performance of pupils inevitably, resulted in a large number of dropouts. For example, in the Aduku community in Sagbama LGA of Bayelsa, the only primary school has been closed down due to lack of teachers (Akinola 2009b:85). Statistics confirmed that attendance at primary school is 43.3 per cent, secondary school 43.2 per cent, while post-secondary education is 13.5 per cent (FGN 2008:225).

As the seventh-largest producer of oil and gas in the world, and the largest in Africa, the Niger Delta contributes over 40 per cent to Nigeria's GDP, about 90 per cent of total annual earnings and about 80 per cent of the national gross income (FGN, 2008:212). In spite of its strategic economic importance, the demographic picture of the region is disturbing. The Human Development Index[2] (HDI) shows deplorable conditions in the Niger Delta as low as 0.453. This figure is lower than regions and nations with the same oil and gas resources, such as Norway (0.963), the United Arab Emirates (0.849), Kuwait (0.844), Libya (0.799), Venezuela (0.772), Saudi Arabia (0.772) and Indonesia (0.697) (Human Development Index Report, 2009[3]).

An important missing element in the conduct of public affairs in the region by the governments, oil companies, and other agencies is the involvement of women and their institutions. Consequently, the misuse of public resources, corruption, and low accountability of government officials in the region continues. The marginalized people of oil-producing

---

[2] The Human Development Index is a standard measure of well-being, encompassing longevity, knowledge and a decent standard of living in terms of access to safe and clean water, quality of health and educational services, electricity, roads, gainful employment, political participation, and the rule of law, etc. It is measured with 1 being the highest ranking score

[3] http://www.nationmaster.com/graph/eco_hum_dev_ind-economy-human-development -index (Accessed 25/06/2009).

communities—whose poverty rate (measured as the share of the population subsisting on less than $1 per day) increased from close to 36 per cent in 1970 to just less than 70 per cent in 2000—have not received benefits from oil-windfall revenues, estimated cumulatively to total US$350 billion (Ogon, 2005; Akinola, 2008b:94). At the same time, the environment is degraded and source of livelihood is affected. What a double tragedy. Since our analysis has shown that women were not involved in all the dubious dealings discussed, and that results of other studies have confirmed the resilience of women in development, we feel strongly that women should be given opportunities. Ownership of oil property should be shared by all the stakeholders—including women, youth and children. Shares could be bought for them. If ownership is shared, then decision-making will also be shared. Inevitably, vandalism will be halted.

Women Organization and Development

Women worldwide work in farms and manage a wide variety of small and micro-businesses, which range from food processing and trading to a multitude of artisan and cottage industry pursuits. Their enterprise and business acumen are renowned and represent tremendous potential for spurring development and resolving social crises at the local level. For instance, the gender dimension of ownership distribution of informal manufacturing enterprises in Nigeria shows that, on average, while the sector is heavily dominated by women (63.4 per cent), the male counterpart accounts for 36.6 per cent. Similarly, the food, beverages and tobacco sub-sector was dominated by females, with 82.7 per cent (Central Bank of Nigeria, 2001). This point to the fact that many Nigerian women have sought a livelihood in the informal sector since wage employment system and the legal trading arrangement has eluded them.

Women throughout Africa have realized that what they cannot accomplish alone is possible when they organize themselves into co-operatives. In this regard, the activities of women groups in countries such as Niger, Senegal, Kenya and Nigeria are well documented (Olowu et. al., 1991; African Farmer, 1992; Awotona and Akinola, 1996). Thus, they are, through united efforts, gradually surmounting their difficulties: providing piped water, playing a key role in communal fundraising and attracting assistance from many international agencies. Women's Participation in Grassroots Development (WPGD) was formed by 10 women in Lewabu community, an area outside Bo, Central Sierra Leone, for the purpose of post-war reconstruction and rehabilitation of victims of rape, widowed and orphaned children. The membership has grown from 10 to 100 women and continues to grow, creating an avenue for self-sustainability (Kreager, 2009:4).

Another example is the Musiri Friends Women Group, Vihiga in Kenya that wants to succeed and determines to put enough food on the table for their families. Due to numerous challenges that these women face (declining tillable land, food shortages, etc), they decided to come together as church women to form this group to engage in productive economic trade activities in order to improve their living standards and the education of their children. The women of Musiri have been engaging in a merry-go-round, a savings pool that the women establish by contributing a mutually agreed upon amount monthly. This pool is used by the women for such needs as school supplies for the children, health issues or financial emergencies in a member's family. The members who receive loans from the merry-go-round pool repay their loan with interest. The majority of the members are already practicing small-scale businesses and have the knowledge and skills to succeed (Kreager, 2009:5).

Similarly, Bidike Village Meeting Women's Group, Kenya embarked on various income-generating projects. The group was originally founded in 1995 as a social and spiritual fellowship with four members. It was officially registered in 2002 with twelve members, with the goal of alleviating poverty and improving their members' living standards. They have access to loans and also engage in an exposure visit to a successful project. The group engages in a merry-go-round. The report shows that the group is well coordinated with energetic women, determination and focus. The project is in the large scale farming area of Kitale. However, it was found that the group needs training on book-keeping to improve their financial record-keeping (Kreager, 2009:8).

According to the World Bank (1997:2), women leading rotating savings and credit associations (ROSCAs) constituted 80 per cent in Nigeria, 57 per cent in Tanzania and 46 per cent in Ghana. Olowu et al. (1991) found that ROSCAs in Nigeria hold elections and remove leaders from office if need be. Most of them have neither written constitutions nor bye-laws. They are bound by faith and trust with rules and regulations written in their minds and these guide their operations. The condition for membership of this type of association was the ability of the individual to fulfill all the financial obligations like daily, weekly or monthly contributions, as the case may be. Awotona and Akinola (1996) show that women's organizations (cooperatives and community development associations) across Nigeria performed significantly in the delivery of public goods and services to their respective communities and the entire development process of their communities. Notwithstanding, women's organizations in Nigeria are few; they are limited in number, hence, the need for more groups to step up and face the numerous challenges. The few that do exist are not without some problems, which require thorough diagnosis and solutions. There is always room for improvement and strengthening.

Indications from South Africa and Zimbabwe corroborate earlier findings. The Zenzele women's clubs of the Eastern Cape of South Africa, which date from the late 1920s, improved the lives of rural African women by enhancing their subsistence farming and cooking skills and educating them about household cleanliness, basic child care, and health care. The associations later spread to places like Uganda, Tanganyika and Southern Rhodesia where they catered for rural women and focused on community development (Higgs, 2004). Similarly, grassroots women groups in Zimbabwe are predominantly self-help that have grown out of local conditions to meet the specific needs of women. These voluntary associations provide services and engage in welfare activities such as offering training in basic skills, support networks, and operating childcare facilities (Chazan et. al., 1988:89).

Okotoni and T. Akinola (2008) found that 85.7 per cent of socio-economic projects in the Ile-Ife region in southwest Nigeria, were planned and executed by women's organizations without any external assistance, while only 4.8 per cent received assistance from government. This establishes the fact that women's organizations have demonstrated their usefulness and indispensability to their communities materially, socially, economically and politically. The productive roles that women's organizations play in grassroots development cannot be overemphasized. Women's organizations possess tremendous potential for stimulating and sustaining grassroots development in Nigeria.

Developmental Role of Niger Delta Woman

The situation of the Niger Delta woman is a true reflection of what entails in the typical Nigerian community. In the rural Niger Delta community, the voice of the woman is not heard at all, nor are her views considered, in spite of her enormous economic contributions in the community. The bulk of the economic activities in the community, i.e. trading, farming and even fishing, are carried out by her. She contributes to paying for community development projects, but how the monies collected are expended she does not know, and does not even have a right to know or ask. Her duty in the community is to take care of the home and raise the children. In spite of all these responsibilities, the Niger Delta woman is not seen as capable or competent enough to be considered for governance, and her views are not good enough to be considered in the decision making process even though bulk of the so called bright ideas being raised by husbands have the input of their wives, directly or indirectly.

Women, as mothers that bear the brunt of the hardship in the villages, are more 'moderate' in their 'reasoning'. They are exempted in matters of plundering and pillage. While others are busy arguing based on selfish interests, women are more concerned with the success of projects that will reduce their burden and that of the children. Once a project is proposed, women begin to prepare for such a project because they know that projects attract money to the community especially during construction. They make money through sales of various foods, drinks and other materials needed by the construction workers. It is important to mention here that the Niger Delta women are very hard working and industrious. They are really nice, and accommodating, and are generally more truthful.

These women, under self-organized arrangements, are playing a significant role in the socio-economic development of their communities. For example, the healthcare project in Tai LGA between 1994 and 1995 was initiated by the women, popularly known as Kawa's Forum. It was a three-year plan, at an estimated cost of NGN 5.0 Million. Initially, a launching was conducted, and NGN 531,000 was realized from within the community and the local government. The breakdown of the contributions is as follows: youths, NGN 15,000; men, NGN 95,000; women, NGN 205,000; elders, NGN 64,000; chiefs, NGN 52,000; and local government, NGN 100,000. The total contributions were NGN 5,332,435 (see Table 7-1), which exceeded the projected amount of NGN 5.0 Million by NGN 332,435. Inflation did not permit the construction of the five planned bungalows, but three bungalows, each having eight rooms, *were* completed. The cottage maternity clinic now child delivery and primary healthcare services in the LGA (see Akinola 2008b:101).

Looking at the breakdown of the amount raised during launching, the women's contribution accounts for 38.6 per cent, while the remaining 61.4 per cent were contributed by other groups in the following order: (a) local government (18.8 per cent), (b) men (17.9 per cent), (c) elders (12.0 per cent), (d) chiefs (9.8 per cent) and (e) youth (2.8 per cent). It is amazing to find that local government that regularly receives colossal amount from oil via federal transfer contributed less than a half (48.7 per cent) of what women contributed.

Table 7-1: Kawa's Annual Contribution toward Maternity Home in Naira (1994–1996)

Year	*Kawa's contribution*	*Kawa's per cent*	*Local Govt.*	*LGA's per cent*	*Total*
1994	413,500	77.5	120,000	22.4	533,500
1995	520,420	61.9	320,950	38.1	841,370
1996	2,417,250	61.0	1,540,315	38.9	3,957,565
Total/Average	3,351,170	62.8	1,981265	37.2	5,332,435

Source: Local Government Annual Report, July 1999, Saakpenwa, River State.

Furthermore, the activities of women in Aduku community in Sagbama LGA of Bayelsa State are highly commendable. Women take care of market maintenance, while the young girls between the ages of 8 and 15 years are in charge of environmental sanitation of the community. The young girls in Aduku community perform the task of environmental sanitation on daily basis. The leader, who normally wakes up her colleagues as early as six o'clock on weekdays and seven o'clock on weekends, moves from street to street or house to house and gathers other girls with a gong at the community square, where the assignments will be distributed. On weekdays, they sweep all the streets in the community before they go to school, while they attend to shrubs and grasses on Saturdays. This suggests that right from their early years, these girls have imbibed the culture of sacrifice, community attachment, patriotism, and for some of them, leadership. If women are performing in voluntary platforms, as shown in the Niger Delta and elsewhere, it is imperative to involve them in the governance of community affairs and developmental projects in their communities.

The above discussions on women in the Niger Delta and Africa confirm that there is a vibrant women's associational life in African societies with a strong sense of community among diverse peoples of Africa. It is in this light that Sills (1959), about four decades ago, predicted that since a considerable body of research and experience has demonstrated that voluntary/mutual associations in diverse communities have accomplished specific purposes, so why can't they be utilized as instruments of planned change? The type of trust and cooperation that local people have instituted among themselves to confront their daily challenges reinforces the notion that the people represent a formidable force necessary to drive changes and transformation to better human societies (see for instance, Akinola, 2008b:103). The question then is: how do we empower this group socio-economically and politically and then harness their developmental potential towards development and peace building in the Niger Delta? This question brings us to the next section, where we discuss the strategy of making the commons work through women associations.

Women Association as a Stabilizing Factor in Grassroots Development in the Niger Delta

Since the working of the commons[4] needs the participants[5] to work together as colleagues in development arenas, the role of women that cuts across all sectors of the economy in the Niger Delta is critical if development is to be achieved. It is on this note that this paper attempts at modelling institutional arrangements that will help to mainstream women's entrepreneurial capability in the development process in the region. Since information asymmetry is one of the factors that strengthen the "prisoner's dilemma", and consequently the "tragedy of the commons", conscious efforts need to be made to ensure a free flow of information—information symmetrical—among the participants. In order to enhance a free flow of information among the development actors in the Niger Delta, an African Polycentric Information Networking (APIN) should be adopted for creating information networks between the leaders and the people on the one hand, and for strengthening linkages and interactions between individuals and self-governing institutions (Akinola, 2008p:188-189, 2011e:67). The beauty of polycentricity is in its multifarious connections and interactive links that all members of a particular community have to receive information interactively and make contributions to decision-making, development and conflict resolution. For example, decisions taken or information passed in a polycentric system have the possibility of reaching every member of a community through at least four of eight channels. Each of the eight associations (occupation, religion, neighbourhood, cooperatives, women, youth, unemployed, and ethnic militia) is a channel for information dissemination. Since these institutions naturally draw their members without much difficulty, the linkages and interactions can then be connected to the state structure of

[4] The commons in the Niger Delta comprise (a) oil that produces revenues for the entire nation, (b) forests, and (c) water bodies that constitute biophysical/material conditions.

[5] The participants are the elite (public officials, scholars) and the non-elite (farmers, fishermen, students, traders, etc).

governance. Once established, the networks can be useful at various domains of human interactions in the Niger Delta, from regional to state and then to local/community levels (see also Akinola, 2009b).

Following this are women's empowerment schemes that need to be entrenched in the Niger Delta. Women's empowerment is an essential ingredient and a precondition for eliminating poverty and securing a better society, because the role of women is irreplaceable in development. Empowerment is a process through which individuals acquire the power to think, act freely, exercise choice and use their abilities or talents without any inhibition (Okwechime 2002:205). Empowerment in relation to women has been seen as an act of gaining the ability to do things and increasing awareness of strategy and capacity to act and set their own agenda to change events in a way they lacked previously. Empowerment occurs only through action. It embraces thinking, learning and acting (Freire, 1972:21; UNDP, 1995; Okwechime, 2002; World Bank, 2003).

According to Wikipedia[6] (2008), empowerment is the process of obtaining basic opportunities for marginalized people, either directly by those people, or through the help of non-marginalized others. Empowerment also includes encouraging and developing the skills for self-sufficiency, with a focus on eliminating the future need for charity or welfare in the individuals of the group. This process, though, may be difficult to start and to implement effectively, but several successful examples of empowerment projects that relate to women should serve as inspirations to development planners, policy makers and practitioners.

It is important, therefore, to evolve strategies to assist women to create their own organization, using the rationale that only they, themselves, can know what their own people need most. Government can act as a facilitator to ensure there is justice and fairness. Any attempt by outsiders to control such organizations can actually help to further entrench marginalization. It is a common experience with charitable organizations leading from outside the community to disempowering the community by entrenching a dependence on charity or welfare as the case in refugees' camps. A non-profit group composed of the indigenous people, however, could ensure that their own organization does have such authority and could set their own agendas, make their own plans, seek the needed resources, do as much of the work as they can, and take responsibility and credit—for the success of their projects (or the consequences, should they fail) (see Wikipedia 2008).

---

[6] http://en.wikipedia.org/wiki/Empowerment (accessed 22/09/2008)

Empowerment[7] is probably the totality of the following or similar capabilities: having decision-making power of one's own; having access to information and resources for taking proper decisions; having a range of options from which you can make choices (not just yes/no, either/or); having the ability to exercise assertiveness in collective decision making; having positive thinking on the ability to make changes; having the ability to learn skills for improving one's personal or group power; having the ability to change others' perceptions by democratic means;, involvement in the growth process and changes that are never-ending and self-initiated; increasing one's positive self-image and overcoming stigma; increasing one's ability in discrete thinking to sort out right and wrong.

In short, empowerment is the process that allows one to gain the knowledge, skill-sets and attitude needed to cope with the changing world and the circumstances in which one lives. Women, under organizational umbrellas, can make positive contributions to the proposed Self-Governing Community Assembly (SGCA) for the Niger Delta—for deliberation, collegiality, mutual trust, reciprocity and a shared community of understanding to enable citizens, both elite and non-elite to operate in synergy to collectively achieve socio-economic and techno-political objectives (for details, see Akinola, 2010a).

Organizations also help women to secure access to credit for consumption and production. The establishment of new and strengthening of existing micro-credit mechanisms and micro-finance institutions should be undertaken so that the outreach of credit is enhanced. For example, Samuel[8] (2009) shows that people's entrepreneurship and voluntary initiatives have demonstrated that people's initiatives, propelled by passionate vision and the courage of conviction, can be inspiring and innovative, with greater transformative potential. These ideas have proved that people's capabilities, beyond the conventional boundaries of State and market, can help herald peace by challenging poverty, inequality and injustice. Bangladesh has been at the forefront of such innovative experiments and efforts.

The initiatives of BRAC[9], Grameen, Proshika and hundreds of such organisations have played a significant role in helping Bangladesh achieve substantive social and human development in less than 30 years. BRAC

---

7 http://en.wikipedia.org/wiki/Empowerment (accessed 22/09/2008)

8 http://www.morungexpress.com/analysis/38811.html (Accessed 3/12/2009)

9 The Bangladesh Rehabilitation Assistance Committee (BRAC), founded in Bangladesh in 1972, is a development organization dedicated to alleviating poverty by empowering the poor to bring about change in their own lives. Its activities and operations cover Asia, Africa and America.

has become one of the largest NGOs in the world, spreading to different parts of Asia and Africa and providing employment to almost 100,000 people. For example, Grameen has proved that poor women are creditworthy, and the bank has become the most well-known brand for microcredit in the world. There is no denying that Grameen has initiated a development model that has helped relatively poor women increase their incomes incrementally. Many organisations such as SEWA (the Self-Employed Women's Association) and thousands of self-help groups in India and other parts of the world have used microfinance as an effective tool to boost the income levels and market capability of relatively poor women.

To be specific, a group of marginalized women in a western Indian city set up a company to manufacture plastic bags. The story of these women changed when they met a social activist who suggested that they should start a women's savings group (WSG) in their locality to be able to save money and utilize it in the form of rotating loans among members. After about five years, the association progressed very well and this unique story of self-empowerment took shape in the form of a company that was set up at a cost of Rs10 million in Talawade. The 160 women who are owners of this company have come together under the ægis of the Swamini Mahila Bachat Gat Akhil Sangh (SMBGAS)—the apex body of various women's small savings groups in the Pimpri Chinchwad Municipal Corporation (PCMC) area. They signed a contract of seven years with a firm called Sumedh Polymers, which will export their plastic bags to Dubai. The raw material is supplied by this company and the women provide the finished goods as per the quality specifications laid down by the firm. Dividends on this investment are paid out to these women. Such an initiative has obviously delighted the women, especially those that have been selling plastic bags for 25 years, and who have now become the part-owners of a company that manufactures polythene sheets, plastic bags and tarpaulin sheets (Huned Contractor, 2009).

In view of the critical role of the Niger Delta women in the agriculture and allied sectors, as producers, concentrated efforts should be made to ensure that the benefits of training, extension and various programmes reach them. The training programmes in soil conservation, social forestry, dairy development and other occupations allied to agriculture like horticulture, livestock including small animal husbandry, poultry, fisheries, etc., should be expanded to benefit Niger Delta women. Since the important role played by women in food processing and agro-industry and textiles has been crucial to the development of these sectors, they should be given comprehensive support. If women are given opportunities to think through problems, discuss and learn from others, and consequently act with other groups in society, they will have strong confidence in the system. The empowerment will give them a voice and confidence in self-governing community assembly. Thus, they, as a group, will become active agents of deliberation on planning and execution of development projects. As a matter of fact and urgency, the Niger Delta women should be involved in the post-amnesty plan and development process.

Polycentric Arrangement and Implementation Strategy for Engaging Women in the Niger Delta Development

What this paper is recommending is similar to the Irepodun project, but with women's groups as a focus. Since women have been identified with substantial contributions in farming, trading, informal manufacturing enterprises (as discussed earlier) they should use organizational platforms to pool together their potential for economic empowerment and poverty reduction in the Niger Delta. In the area of leadership, Nigerian women are not left behind, and in Africa they have made significant strides in the political arena over the past few years (Africa Renewal 2005:6). The implementation strategy is rooted in two factors:

1. The Niger Delta women possess a tremendous institutional capacity to organize themselves for the full utilization of micro-credit facilities and natural resources within their localities;
2. The Niger Delta women, in their organizational setting, constitute formidable economic driver at the local level. If they were organized in a polycentric manner, micro-credit would be judiciously utilized.

Using a polycentric approach, all existing women groups and associations at the local level in the Niger Delta should be identified, brought together under women economic empowerment forum. From this forum, some decisions would be taken on what women can do together and how they can accomplish the task.

Micro-credit can be channelled to these groups as their needs arise from a feasibility study of their proposal. Under this arrangement, the diversion of loans fund ceremonies such as marriage and funerals would be difficult. In a polycentric system, the beneficiary groups benefit from economies of scale. For instance, the processing of a loan normally involves certain stages which cannot be compromised. But if ten women jointly process a loan, they save a lot of money and time as compare with ten of them processing the loan individually. Similarly, the problem of information asymmetry by lenders is resolved in a polycentric system, as the people (lenders and borrowers) exhibit a shared community of understanding.

According to Akinola (2005g), the implementation strategy of this proposal is highlighted under the following 9 steps.

First Step (Adoption of the proposal for implementation)
Experiences of women's institutions in the Niger Delta on rule-ruler-ruled relationships in meeting common challenges need to be taken into consideration in evolving women's economic empowerment. If the participants of this conference agree on this proposal, there is the need for the adoption of the position of this paper.

Second Step (Women's Economic Revival Forum to be held)
The Women's Economic Revival Forum will bring together representatives of all the existing women's groups across the Niger Delta or a state (depending on the scale of implementation). At this forum, this proposal will be presented and unfolded to the representatives. Inputs from participants will be added to the proposal. The official language of the proposed programme will be the mother tongue of the people or, pidgin (local) English.

Academia, government officials (in Agriculture and Commerce & Industry) and some representatives of various women's institutions should: (a) highlight the capacity and potential of, and constraints on, women; (b) make an inventory of natural resources within the geo-political area; and (c) discuss the feasibility of certain medium-scale industries (in specific areas such as food processing—yam flour, cassava flour, maize, fruits, etc.), poultry, fishery, etc. The essence is to ascertain agro-based industrial potentials for transforming farm crops into processed and semi-finished products for local consumption and export.

Third Step
The focus of the third step will be a decision on pilot projects, which should be established in one or two communities. In each community, with input from scholars and government officials, representatives of women's organizations will decide on the type of industry they want to establish and the organizational structure of their proposed enterprise.

Fourth Step

In each community, all the groups will work together and form three committees: Economic Planning Committee, Implementation Committee, and Monitoring Committee. The task of the committees would include: (i) what women can do together (common-pool resources); (ii) ownership of such enterprises—jointly owned by women through shareholding; (iii) the cost and execution of projects, and (iv) monitoring of the projects.

Fifth Step

It is proposed that the Local Government Council (LGC) in a particular area should have some shares in the proposed industry(ies), but not dominate the ownership. The LGC should not own more than 15 per cent of the total shares.

Sixth Step

This is the practical implementation stage for the proposal.

Seventh Step

The evaluation stage of the pilot projects will commence some months after the implementation. The evaluation will be carried out by a group of experts—scholars, few professionals and Local Government officials—and women representatives (selected shareholders, and workers in the new industries).

Eighth Step

Project revision will commence after the evaluation. Here, all lessons from the pilot projects will be used to improve the future design of the projects.

Ninth Step

The last step is concerned with project replication of projects across the Niger Delta. It is suggested that Local Government, along with women groups/associations, industrialists and individuals, should proceed with establishing their firms and industries, which should be jointly owned through shareholding. The implementation strategy is expressed diagrammatically in Figure 7- 1.

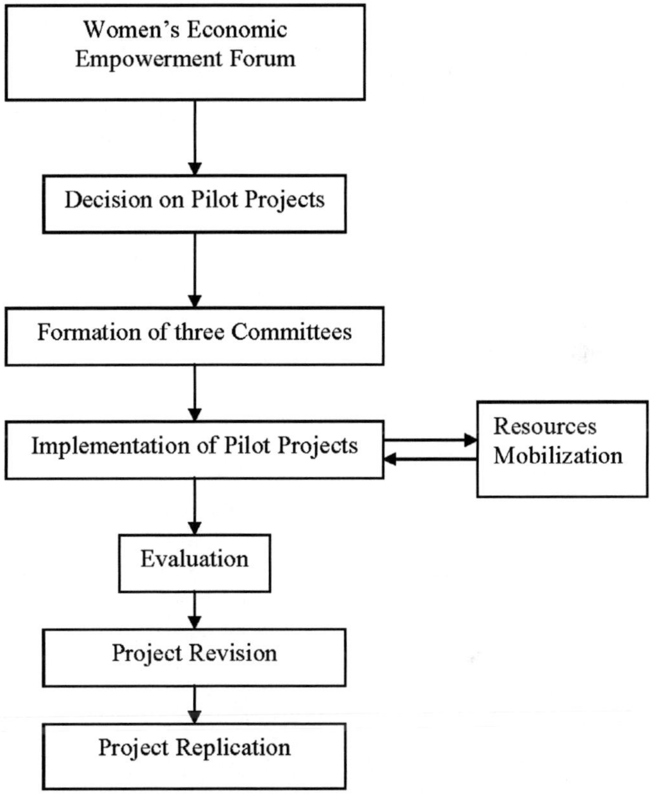

Fig. 7-1: Diagrammatic Expression of the Implementation Strategy
Source: Akinola (2005g)

Mainstreaming Women's Organizations in Socio-Economic and Techno-Political Decision Making in the Niger Delta

The success of empowerment schemes in the Niger Delta will put women on a pedestal, letting them make a meaningful contribution in the proposed SGCA. It is in the light of this that an attempt is made to design a Niger Delta Women's Empowerment and Mainstreaming Model (NDWEMM) (see Fig. 7-2). The first part of the model demonstrates the crisis and tragedy in the commons in the Niger Delta as exhibited by the present arrangement that emphasizes non-renewable resources (oil) at the expense of renewable resources (forests and water bodies). Beside the benefits from oil that are skewed against the people, the impact of oil exploration on forests and water bodies is fast eroding economic base of farmers and fishermen respectively. This is a double tragedy for these groups in the commons! Consequently, the support for food production is eroded by oil spills and gas flaring on forests and water bodies. The implication of all these is a heightened importation of food and dependency syndrome. Inevitably, investment is reduced, the future is bleak for the people, and aggression and crises take their tolls in the region.

The second part of the model focuses on women's empowerment. The model identifies four imperatives that are a sine qua non of women's empowerment: (a) women's organizations, (b) microfinance, (c) women's entrepreneurship and (d) family capability. In order to accomplish women's empowerment, according to the model, four major stakeholders/participants in the public terrain—public officials (politicians, bureaucrats, technocrats), scholars, multinationals and citizens (including women)—need to operate in synergy through a public sphere restructuring mechanism (see for details, Akinola 2010a). The NDWEMM targets an inclusive system that will be self-organizing, self-governing and self-regulating through the use of the IAD.

The restructuring process will commence, first, with the setting up of a self-governing community assembly (SGCA) where participants through their institutions (governments with their agencies, oil companies, higher institutions, community institutions, women organizations) can operate in synergy. The second step is a value re-orientation among scholars, public officials and other participants. This new orientation, invariably, determines: (a) the ability of scholars to take theories to the streets and apply them for the benefit of the citizenry; (b) the synergy between and among scholars and public officials in executing socio-economic and techno-political projects; (c) the relevance and indispensability of community self-governing institutions in decision making; and (d) the centrality and imperativeness of community assembly for decision making and resolution of crisis.

Next, the participants would operate using rules that are crafted by members at the SGCA. Rule-crafting takes place at three levels—constitutional, collective choice, and operational. At the constitutional level lies the system that determines how rules are made and can be modified. At the heart of effective governance of Niger Delta is the imperativeness of constitutional reform (Akinola, 2006c,e), which can be accomplished through pragmatic experience, for example, polycentric privatization and local industrialization. The effectiveness of this strategy has been proved in the Irepodun experiment (Akinola, 2007f:230). Women's organizations should be directly involved in community assembly and jointly take decision on how resources (financial and natural) are to be allocated and utilized. At the collective choice level, rules that define and constrain the actions of individuals and citizens have to be established. At the operational level, concrete actions have to be undertaken by those individuals most directly affected, or by public officials (McGinnis, 1999a).

The outcome of the restructuring is the emergence of new institutional arrangements, which would reflect integrative constitutional order in socio-economic and techno-political realms. It is this joint action and synergy by the four groups (scholars, public officials, oil workers and representatives of community self-governing institutions) that would eventually determine how government policies in all spheres of life are to be implemented. After the institutional arrangement has been designed, an operational strategy for the implementation of any programme/project (e.g. employment generation, food security, road development, poverty reduction, environmental management, electoral reform and democratization, security of life and property, conflict detection, prevention and resolution, etc.) can then be fashioned (see Akinola, 2007f; 2008b,p; 2009a,f; 2010a, 2011i).

Implementation Options

This paper generates two options on the implementation of the ideas contained in this paper:

Option A—Government can implement through NDDC.

Option B—Based on experience, Nigerian governments, in their present structure, may not be able to adopt these strategies because of secrecy and ulterior motives. The reason is that nearly all these ideas have been sent to Nigerian governments and their agencies in the Niger Delta from 1992 to date, but their responses have been appalling and dampening. For example, no fewer than twenty-three attempts have been made to convey problem-solving proposals to the Nigerian governments, either physically or by courier service. As a matter of fact, between October and December 2009, a proposal titled, "Post-Amnesty Plan, Peace-Building and People-Centred Development in the Niger Delta: A Polycentric Planning and Poverty Reduction Strategy (PPPRS)" was sent via courier to: (1) The

President (28 October, 2009), (2) the Vice-President, (3) the Secretary to the Federal Government of Nigeria (28 October 2009), (4) the Group Managing Director, NNPC (4 November 2009), (5) the Group Managing Director, Shell Petroleum Development—SPDC (24 November 2009), (6) the Chairman, Niger Delta Development Commission (NDDC) (8 December 2009), and (7) all the six governors of the South-South Zone (28 December 2009) (with proof of delivery) (see Akinola, 2009h, 2011e). As at the time of preparing this paper, only the NDDC had responded. The suggestion, therefore, is that instead of waiting for government and oil companies, some NGOs, scholars, patriotic individuals, community leaders, etc., can spearhead the implementation of these strategies on a pilot scale. This does not mean, however, that community-orientated projects will succeed no matter what. Successful governance arrangements are often characterized by cooperation at several levels. The outcome of pilot projects will enlighten the people as to how to address the challenges in the region, and in the long run, people will be able to exert their demands on the elected officials.

Conclusion

This chapter concludes that most development projects in the Niger Delta failed because women are not involved right from planning to implementation. This is because, in spite of the positive impact of women's associations on the Niger Delta communities, they (the women) have not been accorded their rightful position in formal decision-making, where they could demonstrate their full potential towards developmental activities and governance of community affairs. Until the Niger Delta people see oil as a common pool resource (as the people of Alaska did) they cannot collectively determine their own destiny.

The chapter found that women, as mothers that bear the brunt of the hardship in the villages, are more 'moderate' in their 'reasoning'. They are exempted in matters of plundering and pillage. In order to make the commons work, this paper, therefore, argues for the involvement of women's organizations in decision-making and the implementation of development projects in the Niger Delta. For them to be able to play this role, they need to be empowered socio-economically so that they can have a voice and confidence in the proposed self-governing community assembly. The paper, therefore, uses the IAD framework to chart possible courses of action to empower, integrate and mainstream women into formal decision-making arrangements in the Niger Delta.

CHAPTER EIGHT

CONCLUSION: ADDRESSING DEFICITS IN GOVERNANCE; THE PATH TO DEVELOPMENT IN THE NIGER DELTA

IBABA SAMUEL IBABA

The discourse on the development deficits in the Niger Delta has identified several causal factors, ranging from the ethnic character of the Nigerian State and the resultant ethnicity-based political domination; the country's centralized federalism and the suffocation of minority ethnic groups; oil induced environmental degradation and the destruction of local economies; ineffective environmental protection laws, corruption, and the misapplication/mismanagement of public funds (Naanen, 1999; Okoko, Nna and Ibaba, 2006; Ibaba, 2009; Ikporukpo, 2011). But Ikelegbe (2011, p. 241) has noted that the explanations have focused on externalities, as emphasis has been placed on the roles of the Nigerian (federal) government and the TOCs, while governance deficits in the region, which is part of the fundamentals that underlie underdevelopment, have been neglected. This concluding chapter shares this view, and makes a case that addressing governance deficits in the Niger Delta is a fundamental requirement for the development of the region. Ikelegbe links the resolution of governance deficits to the 're-orientation of leadership, the institution of good governance practices, the strengthening of citizen participation, and the entrance of quality and competent officials into the governance terrain and the institution of accountable and efficient resource management systems' (p. 242). Agagu (in this volume) has also emphasized the reinvention of public through ethical reform as a solution to governance deficits and promotion of development in the region. Similarly, Onuoha and Ezirim (in this volume) highlight transparency, accountability and lack of corruption in governance as key practices that drive development, while Akinola, Isidahomhen and Akinola (in this volume emphasize policy reforms to integrate women in decision-making. Also, Tamuno and Udom (in this volume) have highlighted the importance of public sector and budgetary reforms to efficient service delivery by government. This chapter agrees with all of these, but argues that the issue of quality and competent leadership, and disciplined character in particular, are central to addressing the constraints to development in the region.

In chapter three of this volume, for example, Onuoha and Ezirim discussed the resource curse, and provided an intelligent background to the development problems in the Niger Delta by linking it to the development challenges in Nigeria. But it is imperative to note that the mere availability of resources does not result in resource curse. Among other factors, character deficiency of leaders defines resource use and management, transparency, accountability, and corruption in governance. This chapter thus interrogates the psychological substrate of the custodians of political power in the Niger Delta, by focusing on the interface between sociopathic personality and governance deficits in the Niger Delta, an issue that has been overlooked in the literature. The chapter makes the point that failure of governance, which has resulted in the poor state of development in the Niger Delta, cannot be dissociated from having sociopaths in government. It does not put the whole blame of the development plight of the region on sociopaths in government, but the objective of the chapter is to highlight the fact that public officers who have sociopathic personalities are linked to poor service delivery by government; and addressing this is crucial for governance reforms.

Sociopathic personality is the outcome of antisocial personality disorder (APD), which refers to “pervasive pattern for, and violation of, the rights of others”. It is noted to “begin in childhood or early adolescence and continues into adulthood”, and is partly caused by the lack of parental affection and discipline and environmental factors (APA, 1994). In the Niger Delta, the long-standing depravation and depredation by the government at all levels (Federal, State, and Local) have created conditions for the development of sociopathic personalities. Individuals with sociopathic personality are characterized by the inability to form warm interpersonal relationships; the lack of feelings of guilt and disregard for family and community values; egocentrism, lack of foresight, and absence of moral judgment; and limited capacity for love, emotional immaturity, excessive dependence on others and poor planning for self development (Olumati, 2006). Individuals with such personality traits see the state as an institution of hate and oppression, and society as an irritant.

They thus see the state and society as objects to be cheated for personal gain or retrieval of what the state and society have denied them. In the Niger Delta this is captured by the common saying among public office holders: "this is our time to chop", meaning, this is our time to take from society and government. In this context, public policies and decisions are made to drive private interests, as against the public interest.

Sociopathic Politics and the Challenge to Good Governance

This section explores the argument that the involvement of sociopaths in governance results in "sociopathic politics", which pursues private interests and thus undermines the capacity of the state to promote the common interests of society. This, the paper argues, partly explains the personalization of the state noted to be a fundamental constraint to good governance and development in Nigeria (Ekekwe, 1986); Ake, 2001; Aaron, 2006). In this context, the chapter interrogates the character deficiency of leadership and its implications for leadership recruitment and governance. Further, it provides insight into the collapse of discipline and social responsibility, which, this chapter argues, partly explains the abuse of office (such as the looting of the public purse and the collusion between electoral officials and politicians to rig elections) for personal gain, actions that undermine democracy, good governance and development. The literature has identified the absence of democracy and good governance as fundamental constraints to development. One such study has provided empirical evidence to make the point that Africa is underdeveloped because of its lack of good governance:

> Comparing the 176 most democratic leaders since 1952… the average democratic leader produced a real annual economic growth rate of 3.04 per cent, compared to 1.78 per cent for the average autocrat. Within Africa … The difference in political openness between the most democratic and the least democratic African state is associated with a growth gap of over 4.5 per cent points per year… One reason why Africa continues to lag so far behind economically is that it lags well behind in governance (Diamond, 2005, p. 6)

No doubt this point is valid. But it is also crucial to note that the absence of democratic governance does not on its own inhibit development: it is either predicated on other factors or interacts with other conditions. Ake (1994, 1996, & 2001) has blamed the failure of democracy, good governance, and development in Africa on the character of the state which rules out politics of moderation and encourages extremism, abuse of power and instability. The custodians of state power use it to pursue private and sectional interests, setting on a desperate struggle for political power and the neglect of development. Ekekwe (1991) agrees with Ake, and notes that in the Nigerian case the desperate struggle for power has created instability, repression of political groups and alienation of the population, thus creating a climate that is hostile to investment and productivity. This highlights the point that the pursuit of private interests by political leaders undermines good governance, and by extension development and peace. Diamond (2005) shares this view by noting that "the capacity of the state to function in the service of the public good" is a fundamental requirement for good governance. But Diamond (2005) emphasizes that this relates to "commitment to the public good" by political leaders, and identifies the sources of this commitment as "dedicated and charismatic leadership, a cultural ethic that appreciates and a structure of institutional incentives that rewards disciplined service to the nation or the general community".

This chapter agrees with the later view expressed by Diamond, but argues that the sociopathic personality undermines the commitment to the public good. Ekekwe (1991) has noted the lack of nationalism, honesty, patriotism and discipline by Nigerian leaders as the fundamental causes of corruption and the failure of development, but did not explain why these virtues are lacking in the leadership. This chapter notes that although it is not limited to it, the lack of these virtues is linked to the effect of the sociopathic personality, and argues that it partly explains why the same Niger Delta leadership that accuses the federal government of neglecting the region turns round to mismanage the financial resources of the area

An essential ingredient of democratic practice is the conduct of periodic free and fair elections to choose leaders. Through elections, the citizens of a country exercise their popular sovereignty, the basis of consent and legitimacy. Significantly, elections in the Niger Delta (Nigeria) are almost always rigged, through the falsification of election results, gerrymandering, manipulation of the voters' register, the commercialization of voting rights, the inflation of votes, or announcing results in places where elections were not held, etc. (Alapiki, 1995; Ibrahim, 2006; Bratton, 2008). These have resulted in what Agbaje and Adejumobi (2006) describe as the travails of electoral politics in Nigeria, as, in their view, votes do not count in Nigerian elections. Although the 2011 general elections were considered to be an improvement on previous elections, the fact remains that voting hardly decides who governs, owing to the commercialization of votes in the electoral process.

Social science literature and institutions such as Human Rights Watch (HRW), have in the recent past, brought the commoditization of violence in the Nigerian electoral process into democratic discourse in the country. The view is that violence is now a commodity bought and sold in the electoral process, as the mobilization and recruitment of armed youths, who are paid on the basis of their fire power to prosecute elections, have become common place (HRW, 2005[a]; Joab-Peterside, 2005). Thus far, this practice, which has turned elections into an armed struggle, has been blamed on politicians, who, because of the privatization and personalization of the Nigerian state, engage in a desperate struggle for political power. In the Niger Delta, this is noted as one of the foundations of militancy. Politicians hired armed thugs to "carry out violence to ensure victory" at elections (HRW, 2005[b]). But the arms provided by the politicians are usually not retrieved, and these were part of the initial arms acquired by militia and cult groups. This suggests that the commoditization of violence in the electoral process (Joab-Peterside, 2005), one effect of sociopathic personality, is a constraint to conflict resolution and development in the region.

One significant outcome of the use of the state for the promotion of private interest is the neglect of development, which has provided push factors for conflict. Poverty and the lack of employment opportunities, two manifestations of development failure, have been noted as factors which have made youths available for manipulation and recruitment as armed political thugs. All in all, a sociopathic personality appears to undermine democracy and good governance, and thus robs the Niger Delta of the development benefits which result from democracy and good governance.

A crucial point to note here is that because sociopaths are self-centred, they tend to use public resources for their comfort when they control political or governmental power. This perspective answers the question, why have the huge oil revenues that have accrued to governments of the Niger Delta not benefited the masses or the majority of citizens who live in poverty? The first chapter has noted the increase in the derivation share of revenue allocation from 3 per cent to 13 per cent in 2000. This change increased the inflow of revenues into the region. The significance of this is better appreciated when compared with the revenue received by other states in the country. In 2008, for instance, out of the total revenue of about $16.5 billion disbursed to the 36 states of the federation, the Niger Delta states alone received over US$7.1 billion (www.fmf.gov.ng). The significance of this huge revenue inflow for analysis on the Niger Delta question is brought to the fore when the revenue inflow into the region is compared with what is received by other states in the country. Available data indicates that the Niger Delta states receive far more revenue than the other states.

In July 2011, for instance, the six Niger Delta states in the South-South geo-political zone received over N211.6 billion, or 34.3 per cent (than one third) of the total revenue of N616,212,843,822.37 that was allocated to the 36 states of the federation and the Federal Capital Territory. Further analysis indicates that the sum received by Akwa-Ibom and Bayelsa States alone was more than that allocated to the South-East geo-political zone made of five states. Again, the amount allocated to Akwa-Ibom, Bayelsa and Delta States was equally higher than the monies received by the North-West geo-political zone made of seven states. Similarly, the monies received by states which got the highest allocations in the other geo-political zones were far less than those received by the Niger Delta States. The allocations show that Anambra State received the highest in the South East zone with N12, 623,612,932.39 (2.0 per cent). Similarly, Lagos in the South-West zone got the highest, with N22, 821,435,409.32 (3.7 per cent). Benue, in the North-Central zone, received N13, 616,448,796.04 (2.2 per cent). Borno, in North-East, and Kano in North–West zones, received N15, 597,584,329.34 (2.5 per cent) and N22, 906,019,625.04 (3.7 per cent) respectively. Despite this huge inflow of revenue, the development indicators are disappointing as noted in the introductory chapter.

The meagre impact of the revenues on the poor suggests that financial resources have not been properly managed and scholars have linked this to the self-serving culture of politics which encourages corruption and neglects the poor in resource allocation. Resource disbursement encourages corruption through huge allocations to overhead costs and capital projects that hardly benefits the poor (Ikelegbe, 2011; Ibaba, 2011). However, political leaders, government functionaries and Niger Delta activists have disputed this, and blamed it on the harsh geographical terrain, which in most cases requires land reclamation before roads and buildings can be constructed. Similarly, the many creeks, rivers and streams necessitate the construction of bridges for road projects; and add to the costs of such projects. To be sure, the cost of providing infrastructure in the Niger Delta is more expensive than other parts of Nigeria. For example, the road construction engineering calculus has put the cost of constructing a kilometre of road in the swamps of the Niger Delta at N10 million, as against N2.5 million in the upland parts of the country (Adeyemo, 2008, p. 82).

However, the numerous charges of corruption against past and serving political office holders by the country's anti-graft agency, the Economic and Financial Crimes Commission (EFCC), which involve billions of naira, do not support this argument. Furthermore, the public expenditure pattern clearly shows a disconnect between the developments of the people and the expenditure preference of the custodians of political power in the region. Available data indicates, for instance, that the combined 2008 budgets of the four states that receive the highest revenues in the region (Akwa-Ibom, Bayelsa, Delta and Rivers) allocated 13.2 per cent and 26.6 per cent respectively to health and education, while the legislative arm of government and Government House (the seat of government excluding the MDAs) received 7.27 per cent and 46.5 per cent (Ibaba, 2011, p. 34). The expenditure for the huge allocations to Government House include security vote, entertainment and hospitality, travels and tours, stationery, utility services, maintenance of furniture and vehicles, and consultancy services. These expenditures, which have no bearing on improving the quality of life of the citizens, end up as a vehicle of deprivation, as they have become avenues for siphoning off public resources by the political leaders.

Significantly, these leaders have joined in the agitations for development and equitable share of oil revenues that triggered the violence in the Niger Delta. The question that arises is, "Why should a leadership that accuses the federal government of neglect and exploitation of the Niger Delta turn round and mismanage the resources of the same people?" The chapter makes the point that the most likely reason is that the leaders have sociopathic traits, particularly a lack of social responsibility, which makes them see their being in government as an opportunity for personal aggrandizement. The deprivation resulting from this has contributed to the exacerbation of underdevelopment. This indicates that addressing the challenges of the sociopathic personality is fundamental to governance reform, which is essential for the correction of governance deficits

Concluding Notes

The discourse in this book indicates that addressing the issue of governance deficits is the most defining policy strategy to ensure development in the Niger Delta. This requires governance reforms in the critical areas of leadership recruitment, strengthening the capacity of public institutions, and public sector/ budgetary reforms. These are required to ensure that government pursues the common good, as against the present situation where it serves the private interests of the custodians of political power. This is a prescription for all tiers of government, and the focus on sociopathic personality is not meant to overlook these crucial issues, but to draw attention to the fact that sociopaths in government constitute a huge challenge to reforms in governance, and thus the phenomenon needs to be tackled as part of the reform process. In addition to making the aspirations of citizens the primary objective of governance, it would not be out of place for political parties and leadership recruitment agencies to insist on leadership training which emphasize behaviour modification, as a requirement for eligibility.

BIBLIOGRAPHY

Aaron, K.K., Can a Privatized State Privatize? Insights and Experience from Nigeria's Privatization Program. Port Harcourt, Nigeria: Kemuela Publications, 2006.

Abayomi, F., Dotun, A., Matswamgbe, M., Onwumah, U., & Okpewho, L. "Report of Small Arms and Light Weapons (SALW) Survey in Delta State", in *Oiling Violence: The Proliferation of Small Arms and Light Weapons in the Niger Delta. Lagos*, ed. Ibeanu, O. & Mohammed, F.K. Frankard Publishers, 2005.

Abbas, V 'Effect of government capital expenditure on GDP in the Iranian economy using superexogeneity testing', *Applied Economics Letters*, 1466-4291, Volume 5, Issue 6, 1998, Pages 361-364, 1998. http://www.informaworld.com/smpp/content~db=all~content=a713760165. Accessed on 18/12/2009

Abdullahi. A. Corruption the Greatest Obstacle to National Development", in *Nigeria: Corruption in Development.* ed Odekunle, F. Ibadan: Ibadan University Press, 1986.

Abdullateef, U, et al. Budgetary allocations and sectoral contributions to economic development in Nigeria. Department of Accounting and Finance, University of Ilorin, Nigeria, 2008.

Adegoroye, A. 'The Challenges of Environmental Enforcement in Africa: The Nigerian Experience', Third international Conference on Environmental Enforcement Proceedings, 1994.

Adeyemi, O. T. Oil Exploration and Environmental Degradation: the Nigerian Experience, Environmental Informatics Archives, No.2, 2004, pp.387-393

Adeyemi-Suenu, W. & Inokoba, P. "Armed Rebellion and the Future of Self- Determination in the Niger Delta", paper presented at the International Conference on Natural Resource, Security and Development in the Niger Delta, Organized by the Department of Political Science, Niger Delta University, in Collaboration with the Centre for Applied Environmental Research, Department of Geosciences, University of Missouri Kansas City, USA. Yenagoa, Bayelsa State, Nigeria March 8-11, 2010,

Adeyemo, A. "Environmental Policy Failure in Nigeria and the Tragedy of Underdevelopment of Niger Delta Region", University of Port Harcourt, Nigeria, Inaugural Lecture Series (No. 63), 2008

Adeyemo, A.M. "Environmental Policy Failure in Nigeria and the Tragedy of Underdevelopment of Niger Delta Region", Inaugural Lecture No. 63, University of Port Harcourt, 2008

Adeyemo, D., & Olu–Adeyemi, L. "Amnesty in a Vacuum: The Unending Insurgency in the Niger Delta of Nigeria", in *Checkmating the Resurgence of Violence in the Niger Delta*, Ojarokotu, V & Gilbert, L.D. (eds), Johannesburg, 2010, online publication, www.iags.org/Niger_Delta_book_.pdf; accessed on 08/02/2011

African Farmer: The Key to Africa's Future", The Hunger Project, 1992 No. 7.

African Peer Review Mechanism. *Country Review Report: Federal Republic of Nigeria*. South Africa, Africa Peer Review Secretariat, 2008

African Women Battle for Equality. Africa Renewal Vol. 19, No. 2, July, pp. 6-9, 2005

Agagu, A.A., ''Recreating the Nigerian State for Sustainable Higher Education". Proceedings of the Second Regional Conference on Reforms and Revitalization of Higher Education, organized by the Higher Education Research and Policy Network (HERPNET) held at the International Institute of Tropical Agriculture, Ibadan, 13-16 August, 2007.

—. "Corporate Social Responsibility and the Niger Delta Crisis". Proceedings of an International Conference on Meeting Environmental Challenges in the Coastal Region of Nigeria, held at the University of Abertay. Dundee, Scotland, 29.9.2008-1.10.2008.

Agbaje, A. & Adejumobi, S. "Do Votes Count? The Travails of Electoral Politics in Nigeria". Africa Development, Vol. XXXI, No. 3, pp.25-44, 2006.

Agiebenebo, T.J. et al. *Public sector economics: theories, issues and application*. Port Harcourt: K B & I Ltd, 2000.

Ahmad, Z. M & Martha, F. *Women Workers in Rural Development*. Geneva: International Labour Organisation, 1985.

Akanbi, F. "Industry Leaders set Agenda on Sovereign Wealth Funds", This Day News Paper, Lagos, Nigeria, , 16 January, 2011.

Ake, C. *Democratization of Disempowerment in Africa*. Lagos: Malthouse Press Ltd., 1994.

—. "Is Africa Democratising?" in *Crises and Contradictions in Nigeria's Democratic Programme, 1986-1993*. Mimiko, N.O. (ed). Akure: Stebak Ventures Ltd, 1995

—. "The Political Question", in *The Nigerian Political Process.* Alapiki, H.E (ed). Port Harcourt: Emhai Printing and Publishing Company, 2001.

—. *Is Africa Democratizing?* Lagos: Malthouse Press Ltd., 1996.

Akinola, S.R. "Resolving the Niger-Delta Crises through Polycentric Governance in Nigeria", Paper presented at a colloquium organized by the Workshop in Political Theory and Policy Analysis, in Indiana University, Bloomington, USA, December 1, 2003

—. "Local Self-Governance as an Alternative to Predatory Local Governments in Nigeria". International Journal of Studies in Humanities 1(3):47–60. 2004

—. "Structural Transformation and Polycentric Governance: Complementary Strategy towards Nigeria's Reform Agenda". Proceedings of the 14th General Assembly of Social Science Academy of Nigeria, Abuja, Nigeria, pp. 238-250, 2005

—. "Micro-Credit, Women Empowerment and Poverty Reduction at the Local Level: A Polycentric Approach." Workshop organized by Brightlight Management Consultancy for the Osun State Nigerian Union of Local Government Employees (NULGE), Women's Wing at Rialto Hotel, Ojota, Lagos, 15-17 November 2005.

—. "Structural Transformation and Polycentric Governance: A Constitutional Gateway towards Nigerian Democratization". Paper Presented at the Public Hearing for the Review of the 1999 Constitution, The Osun State House of Assembly, Southwest Zone, Osogbo, February 22-23, 2006. The revised version of the paper was presented at a Working Conference on 'Designing Constitutional Arrangements for Democratic Governance in Africa: Challenges and Possibilities', cosponsored by the Workshop in Political Theory and Policy Analysis, African Studies Program, and the Office of International Programs, Indiana University, Bloomington, USA, March 30-31, 2006.

—. "Coping with Infrastructural Deprivation through Collective Action among Rural People in Nigeria". *Nordic Journal of African Studies.* Vol. 16(1) 2007, pp. 30-46, 2007. http://www.njas.helsinki.fi

—. Knowledge Generation, Political Actions and African Development: A Polycentric Approach. *International Journal of African Renaissance Studies*, 2(2):217–238. 2007

—. "Coping With Social Deprivation through Self-Governing Institutions in Oil Communities of Nigeria". *Africa Today* 55(1):89–107, 2008

—. "Alternative Planning Models for Development in Africa". In *Knowledge to Remobilise Africa.* , pp. 169–202. The Development Bank of South Africa (ed), Johannesburg: Knowledge Management Division. 2008

—. "The Failure of Central Policing and the Resilience of Community-Based Security Institutions in Nigeria". In *Civil Society, Governance and Regional Integration in Africa.* Adekunle, Amuwo; Hippolyt A.S; Paul and Irene Omolola Adadevoh, Development Policy Management Forum (DPMF), Nairobi, pp. 257-274. 2009

—. "Polycentric Planning and Community Self-Governance as Panacea to the Niger Delta Crisis". *African Journal of Development (AJD).* New York: New York University, Vol. 11, No. 2, pp. 79-104. 2009

—. "Post-Amnesty Plan, Peace-Building and People-Centred Development in the Niger Delta: A Polycentric Planning and Poverty Reduction Strategy (PPPRS)." Proposal Submitted to: (1) The President, (2) The Vice-President, (3) The Secretary to the Federal Government of Nigeria (October 28, 2009), (4) The Group Managing Director NNPC (November 4, 2009), (5) The Group Managing Director Shell Petroleum Development SPDC (November 24, 2009), (6) The Chairman, Niger Delta Development Commission (NDDC) (December 8, 2009) and (7) all the six Governors of the South-South Zone (December 28, 2009).

—. "Restructuring the Public Sphere for Social Order in the Niger Delta through Polycentric Planning: What Lessons For Africa?" *Journal of African Asian Studies*, Vol. 9, Nos. 1-2, pp. 55-82. Ithaca, NY: Cornell University Press, 2010.

—. "Restructuring the Public Sphere for Democratic Governance and Development in Africa: The Polycentric Planning Approach". In *Political Culture, Governance and the State in Africa*, pp. 1-61. Abdalla Bujra (ed). Nairobi: Development Policy Management Forum (DPMF), 2011

—. "Community Self-Governance as a Panacea for Environmental and Social Injustice in the Niger-Delta of Nigeria". In *Perspectives on African Studies: Essays in Honour of Toyin Falola Akin,* pp. 220- 248. Alao and Rotimi Taiwo (eds.). Munich: LINCOM Europa, 2011.

—. "Post-Amnesty Plan, Peace-Building and People-Centred Development in the Niger Delta: A Polycentric Planning and Poverty Reduction

Strategy (PPPRS)". *Journal of Sustainable Development and Environmental Protection*, Vol. 1, No. 2, pp. 52-75, 2011.

—. "Institutional Analysis, Peasant Farmers and Food Security Paradigm in Africa: A Polycentric Governance and Poverty Reduction Perspective." Paper submitted to *South African Journal of International Affairs*. Braamfontein: The South African Institute of International Affairs, South Africa, 2011.

—. "Balancing the Equation of Governance at the Grassroots" In *People-Centred Democracy in Nigeria? The Search for Alternative Systems of Governance at the Grassroots*, pp. 171–197. ed. Adebayo Adedeji and Bamildele Ayo. Ibadan: Heinemann, 2000

—. "Restructuring the Public Sphere for Social Order in the Niger Delta through Polycentric Planning: What Lessons for Africa?" *Journal of African Asian Studies,* Vol. 9, Nos. 1-2, 2010.

—. Land Use Decree, Forest Administration and Governance Crisis in Nigeria. Promoting Land Administration and Good Governance, 5th FIG Regional Conference, Accra, Ghana, March 8-11 2006.

Ako, R. "Ensuring Public Participation In Environmental Impact Assessment of Development Projects in the Niger Delta Region of Nigeria: A Veritable Tool For Sustainable Development", 3 *Environtropica* 2. 2006.

—. "Resolving the Conflicts in Nigeria's Oil Industry—A Critical Analysis of the Role of Public Participation", PhD thesis submitted to the University of Kent at Canterbury, 2008.

—. "Resource Exploitation and Environmental Justice in Developing Countries: The Nigerian Experience". In *Natural Resource Investment and Africa's Development.* F. Botchway (ed). Cheltenham: Edward Elgar, forthcoming

Akosile, A. "Mass Participation, Antidote to Poverty", *ThisDay*, 16 October, 2007.

Akpan, N. & Akpabio, E. "Youth Restiveness and Violence in the Niger Delta Region of Nigeria: Implications and Suggested Solutions", 2 *International Journal of Development Issues* 2, 37-58, 2003.

Akporido, S.O. Emuobonoviel, I.J. & Akporideo, C.E. "A study of the quality characteristics of surface and underground water in Sapele and Ogharefe Oil producing areas of Delta State". *Nigerian Journal of Science and Environment*. Vol. 2, pp75-86, 2000.

Akwuole, K. "Thinking beyond oil". *The Punch,* 30 October 2006.

Alakpodia, I.J. "The Environment of the Niger Delta". In *Readings in General Studies, Nigerian People and Culture,* pp. 190-203. Uweru B.C. and Ubrurhe J.O. (eds) Warri: About Research Publisher, 2000

Alapiki, H. "Election and Party Preference Index in Nigeria: Analyses of the 1979, 1983 and 1993 Presidential Elections". *Journal of Nigerian Affairs*, Vol. 1., No. 1, pp. 89-97, 1995

Anango, I. 'Environmental Impact Assessment as a Tool for Sustainable Development: The Nigerian Experience', FIG XXII International Congress Washington, D.C. USA, April 19-26 2002. http://www.fig.net/pub/fig_2002/Ts10-3/TS10_3_anago.pdf (accessed 06 March 2012).

Angaye, G. *Petroleum and the Political Economy of Nigeria in The Nigerian Economy: A Political economy approach*. Lagos: Longmans, 1986.

Anon. Niger Delta *Natural Resource Damage Assessment and Restoration* Project. Phase 1– Scoping Report. Federal Ministry of Environment, Abuja Nigeria Conservation Foundation, Lagos, WWF UK, CEESP-IUCN Commission on Environmental, Economic, and Social Policy, 2006.

Anyanwu, J.C. *The Structure of the Nigerian Economy (1960-1997)*. Onitsha: Hybrid Publishers, 1997.

American Psychiatric Association. *Diagnostic and Statistical Manual of Mental Disorders*, Washington, DC: American Psychiatric Association, 1994.

Ashiomanedu, J. "Niger Delta: The Sustainable Development Challenge". *Journal of Sustainable Development in Africa* 11(4): 217-229, 2009

Asonye, C. C & E. R. Bello. "The blight of pollution keratoconjunctivitis among children in oil-producing industrial areas of Delta State, Nigeria". *Ecotoxicology and Environmental Safety*: 59(2):244-248, 2004

Awosika, L. F., French, G. T., Nicholls, R. J. & Ibe, C. E. (1992), *The impact of Sea level Rise on the Coastline of Nigeria.* In: Proceedings of IPCC Symposium on the Rising Challenges of the Sea. Magaritta, Venezuela. 14-19 March, 1992.

Awotona, A. & Akinola, S. R. (1996), "The Participation of Women in Housing and Community Development in Africa: A Case Study of Nigeria". In *Housing Question of the "Others"*, pp.106-115. Emine M. Komut (ed.). Chamber of Architects of Turkey, Ankara, Turkey, 1996.

Bannon, I. & Collier, P. "Natural Resource and Conflict: What we can Do". In *Natural Resources and Violent Conflict: Options and Actions*. Bannon, I. and Collier, P. (eds.) Washington D.C: The World Bank, 2003.

Baqir, R. 'Social sector spending in a panel of countries'. IMF working paper WP/02/35. Washington, DC: International Monetary fund, 2000.

Barbier, E. *Economics, Natural Resource Scarcity and Development.* London: Earthscan Publications Ltd., 1989

Barkan, J. D., M. McNulty, & M. Ayeni. "Hometown Voluntary Associations and Emergence of Civil Society in Western Nigeria". *Journal of Modern African Studies*, Vol. 29, No. 3, pp. 457-480, 1991.

Bayelsa State of Nigeria. *2008 Budget*. Bayelsa State: Budget and Control Department, Ministry of Finance and Budget, Yenagoa, 2008.

Beckman, B. "Political Science and Political Economy". In *Political Science in Africa. A critical Review.* Barongo, Y. (ed). London: Zed Press. 1983

Bertucci, G. *Reconstructing Governance and Public Administration for Peaceful, Sustainable Development*. New York: United Nations. Unpan.org/publicationPDFs/e-libraryarchives/2003 (accessed 8 March 2012)

Birnie, P., Boyle, A. & Redgwell, C. *International Law and the Environment,* 3d ed. Oxford: Oxford University Press, 2009.

Bratton, M. "Vote Buying and Violence in Nigerian Election Campaigns", *Afrobarometer Working Paper*, No.99, 2008

Bromley, Daniel W. (ed.) "The Commons, Property and Common-Property Regimes." In *Making the Commons Work: Theory, Practice and Policy.* pp. 3-15. Bromley, Daniel W. (ed.). San Francisco: Institute for Contemporary Studies, 1992.

Budina, N. & Van Wijnbergen, S. , "Managing Oil Revenue Volatility in Nigeria: The Role of Fiscal Policy". In Go, D and Page, J, *Africa at a Turning Point? Growth, Aid and External Shocks*. Washington, DC: The World Bank, 2008.

Campbell, J. *Nigeria Dancing on the Brink*. Ibaban: Bookcraft, 2010

Cavnar, A. "Case Studies in Oil Governance: What Ghana can learn about Oil Revenue Management from the Rest of the World", *Critical Perspectives No.*23, Ghana Centre for Democratic Development, October 2008.

Central Bank of Nigeria. *Changing Structure of the Nigerian Economy and Economic Implications for Development,* Lagos: Realm Publishers Ltd., 2000.

—. Public finance statistics. Abuja: CBN, 2009

—. (CBN), Federal Office of Statistics (FOS) and Nigerian Institute of Social and Economic Research (NISER): A Study of Nigeria's Informal Sector, Vol. II, Lagos: 2001.

Chandler, C. *The Ghana Story*, London: Linden Press, 1971.

Chazan, Naomi, R. Mortimer, J. Ravenhill, and D. Rothchild. *Policies and Society in Contemporary Africa*. Houndmills: Macmillan, 1988

Collier, P. and Hoeffler, A. "On Economic Causes of Civil War", *Oxford Economic Papers,* No 50, pp.563 – 573, 2002.

Costanza, R. and Wainger, L. (1991)*Ecological Economics, Mending the Earth*. Berkeley: North Atlantic Books, 1991.

Da Coasta, G. "Oil Pollution in Nigeria, www.greenature.com/articles 266.htm. Accessed 15 Sept 2010l.

—. "NigeriaExRebelsProtestoverAllowances."6 September, 2009. http://www.voanews.com/english/2009-09-26-voa31.cfm. Accessed 28/09/2009.

De Rivera, J. "Assessing the Basis for a Culture of Peace in Contemporary Societies". Journal of Peace Research, Vol. 41, No. 5, 2004.

Diamond, L. "Democracy, Development and Good Governance: The Inseparable Links". Paper presented at the Annual Democracy and Governance Lecture, Centre for Democratic Development, The British Council Hall, Accra, Ghana, March 1, 2005.

Dorotinsky, W. 'Capital budgeting and public financial management – Part I & II' published on IMF's PFM blog at http://blog-pfm.imf.org. 2008.

Economic Community of West African States (ECOWAS). *ECOWAS Conflict Prevention Framework.* Abuja: ECOWAS Commission, 2008.

Edoho, F. & Dibie, R. "Executing Environmental Policy and Waste Management in Ghana and Nigeria". *Journal of Sustainable Development in Africa* 2 (2): 38 – 70. 2000.

Efe, S. I. "Urban Effects on Precipitation Amount, Distribution and Rainwater Quality in Warri Metropolis". PhD Thesis in the Dept. of Geography and Regional Planning, Delta State University, Abraka. Nigeria. pp 105-154. 2005.

—. "Quality of Rainwater Harvesting for Rural Communities of Delta State, Nigeria". *The Environmentalist* 26:175-181, 2006.

—. "Environment and Sustainable Development: the case of Climate Change and Flood hazards in The Niger Delta Region of Nigeria". A paper presented at the International Conference on Natural Resource, Security and Development in the Niger Delta held at Niger Delta Wetlands Centre, Yenagoa Bayelsa State, Nigeria, on March 8-11, 2010.

—. "Spatial variation in acid and some heavy metal composition of rainwater harvesting in the oil-producing region of Nigeria". Nat Hazards 55:307–319, 2010.

Efe, S. I. & Mogborukor, J.O.A. "Acid Rain in the Niger Delta region: Implication on Water Resource Crises". A paper presented at the International Conference on the Nigerian State, Oil industry and the

Niger Delta, at Gloryland Cultural Centre, Yenagoa Bayelsa, 11-13 March, 2008.

Efe, S. I. & Mogborukor, J.O.. "Flood Hazards in Warri a Third Word City, Nigeria". *Journal of Social and Management Sciences* 5(2): 83-93, 2010.

Efe, S.I. "Gas Flaring and the Niger Delta Environment. A Climatological Analysis". *African Journal of Environmental studies*. 3(1&2): 11-17, 2002.

—. "Effect of Gas Flaring on Temperature and Adjacent Vegetation in Niger Delta Environment". *International Journal of Environmental issues*. Vol. 1, No. 1: pp. 91-101, 2003.

—. "Urban Flooding in Abraka Delta State, Nigeria". *Journal of Environmental Conservation and Research,* Vol. 1 (2) Pp. 96-103, 2007.

Egonmwan, Johnson A. *Public Policy Analysis: Concepts and Applications*. Benin City: M.O. Aka and Brothers Press, 1991.

Ekekwe, E. "Permanent Crisis in the Nigerian Political Economy", in *Issues in the Political Economy of Structural Adjustment in Nigeria.* Onyeiwu S & Iwarimie-JaJa, D. (eds). Port Harcourt: SIJ Publishers, 1991

—. *Class and State in Nigeria*, Lagos: Longmans, 1986.

Elumilade, D. et al. "Capital budgeting and economic development in the third world: the case of Nigeria", *International Research Journal of Finance and Economics.* ISSN 1450-2887 Issue 2 (2006), Euro Journals Publishing, Inc. http://www.eurojournals.com/finance.htm

Emeseh, E. "The Limitations of Law in Promoting Synergy between Environment and Development Policies in Developing Countries: A Case Study of the Petroleum Industry in Nigeria", 24 *Journal of Energy and Natural Resources Law* 4, 574-606, 2006.

Emeseh, E., Ako, R., Okonmah, P. & Obokoh, L. "Corporations, CSR and Self-Regulation: What Lessons from the Global Financial Crisis?" 11 *German Law Journal* 2, 230-259. Environmental Informatics Archives, 2:387-393, 2010.

Enweremadu, D.U. "The Vicious Circle: Oil, Corruption and Armed conflicts in the Niger Delta". Conference Proceedings, International Conference on the Nigerian State, Oil Industry and the Niger Delta, Organized by the Department of Political Science, Niger Delta University, in Collaboration with the Centre for Applied Environmental Research, Department of Geosciences, University of Missouri, Kansas City, USA. Yenagoa, Bayelsa State, Nigeria, March 11-13, 2008.

Etekpe, A. *Politics of Resource Allocation and Control in Nigeria*. Port Harcourt: Harey Publications Co., 2007.

Ewusi, K. ., *Urbanisation, Modernisation and Employment of Women in Ghana*. Accra: Adwisa Publications, 1987.

Ezekwesili, Obiageli. "Nigerian EITI". In *Transparency Watch*, TI Berlin, July 2006.

Ezirim, G E. "The Political Economy of the Resource Curse and Development in the Gulf of Guinea: Nigeria in Perspective". *International Journal of Modern Political Economy*. Vol. 1. No. 1 (2010), pp. 97-114, 2010.

Ezirim, G.E. & Ifesinachi, K. "Transparency and Governance: A Focus on the Nigerian Extractive Industries Transparency Initiative (NEITI) and the Nigerian Oil Sector". *Nigerian Journal of Humanities and Social Sciences*, (1)2, 2009.

Ezirim, G.E. "Petropolitics and Environmental Criminality in the Niger Delta: Advocacy for Enforcementof Global Conventions". *University of Nigeria Journal of Political Economy*, Vol. 2, Nos. 1&2, 2008.

—. "Saving Ghana from Her Oil: Analyzing the Direct-Cash-Distribution Thesis". *Journal of Politics and Administrative Studies,* Vol. 6, No.2, 2010.

F.B.S. *Annual Abstract and Statistics*. Abuja: Federal office of statistics, 2009.

Fearon, J.D. *Why Do Some Civil Wars Last so Much Longer than Others?* California: Stanford University, Department of Political Science, 2002

Federal Ministry of Finance, Abuja, Nigeria, www. Fmf.gov.ng

FGN (Federal Government of Nigeria), Road Map 2020: Sustainable Development in the Niger Delta – The Master Plan (1960-2007). A Consolidation of Democracy. 1st October Publishing, A Folio/Daily Times Nigeria Publication, Abuja, Vol. 2, 2008

Freire, P. *Pedagogy of the Oppressed*. London: Penguin Books, 1972.

Friends of the Earth International Press Briefing. 'Shell fails to obey gas flaring court order', May 2, 2007 http://www.foe.co.uk/resource/press_releases/shell_fails_to_obey_gas_fl_02052007.html (accessed 29 May 2008).

Fritjof, C. *The Web of Life: A New Scientific Understanding of Living Systems*, (1st edition), New York, Anchor Books/Doubledan, 1996

Frynas, J. *Oil in Nigeria: Conflict and Litigation between Oil Companies and Village Communities*. New Brunswick: Transaction Publishers, 2000.

Fortune News Nov 30, 2010.

www.nigerianbestforum.com/generaltopics/?p=78442/ www.cenbank.org/OUT/PUBLICATIONS/OCCASIONALPAPERS/RD/... (OBADAN)/ faculty.wcas.northwestern.edu/~kmatsu/Poverty%20Traps.pdf

Gelb, A. and Associates. *Oil windfalls: Blessing or Curse*. New York: Oxford University Press, 1998.

Goodland, R. & Ledoc, G. "Neoclassical Economics and Principles of Sustainable Development", 38 *Ecological Modeling*, 19-46, 1987

Gretchen, C.D. *Nature's Services: Societal Dependence on Natural Ecosystem*. Washington, DC: Island Press, pp. 1-40, 1997

Gupta, S. et al. "The efficiency of government expenditure—experiences from Africa". IMF working paper WP/97/153. Washington, DC: International Monetary fund, 1997.

Gupta, S. et al. "Does higher government spending buy better results in education and health care?" IMF working paper WP/99/21. Washington, DC: International Monetary fund, 1999.

Haglund, B.J.A.; Petterson, B.; Finer, D. & Tillgren, P. (eds.). *Creating Supportive Environments for Health*. Geneva: World Health Organisation, 1996

Haveman, R. "Thoughts on the Sustainable Development Concept and the Environmental Effects of Economic Policy". Paper No. 5. Paris: OECD seminar on The Economics of Environmental Issues, Sept. 25, 1989.

Hawkins, Robert B. "Forward". In *Making the Commons Work: Theory, Practice and Policy*. Bromley, Daniel W. (ed.). San Francisco: Institute for Contemporary Studies. pp. xi-xii, 1992.

Higgs, Catherine. "Zenzele: African Women's Self-Help Organizations in South Africa, 1927-1998." *African Studies Review*, Dec 2004. (http://findarticles.com/p/articles/mi_qa4106/is_200412/ai_n10298383. Accessed on 22/07/2007).

Holder, J. & Lee, M. *Environmental Protection, Law and Policy: Text and Materials* (2d ed). Cambridge: Cambridge University Press, 2007.

Holmberg, J. (ed.) *Making Development Sustainable*. Washington, DC: Island Press, 1992.

Hossain, K. "Evolving Principles of Sustainable Development and Good Governance". In *Sustainable Development and Good Governance*. K. Ginther, et al. (eds.) Norwell, MA: Kluwer Academic Publishers, 1995.

HRW (Human Rights Watch). "Rivers and Blood: Guns, Oil and Power in Nigeria's Rivers State". A Human Rights Watch Briefing paper, February 2005.

HRW (Human Rights Watch). "Violence in Nigeria's Oil Rich Rivers State in 2004". A Human Rights Watch Briefing Paper, February 2005

HunedContractor,"Poorwomenturncompanydirectors".*OneWorldSouthAsia*.http://southasia.oneworld.net/fromthegrassroots/poor-women-turn-company-directors (Accessed 10/08/2009).

Hussaini, I. Environmental Impact Assessment Procedures: Seminar presentation at a training workshop organized by Kaduna Environmental Protection Authority quoted in Anago, I., 'Environmental Impact Assessment as a Tool for Sustainable Development: The Nigerian Experience', FIG XXII International Congress Washington, D.C. USA, April 19-26 2002.

Ibaba S.I. "Niger Delta: Interrogating the Peace and Development Nexus". Department of Political Science, Niger Delta University, Monograph Series, No. 5, 2011.

—. "Civil Society Organizations, Democracy and Peace Building in the Niger Delta". *International Journal of Nigerian Studies and Development*, Vol. 15, pp.32-49, 2009.

—. "Poverty Trap and Violent Conflicts in the Niger Delta: Exploring the Implications for Post-Amnesty Peace Building". Paper presented at International Development Research Council (IDRC), Think Tank Initiative (TTI) & Center for Population and Environmental Development (CPED) Workshop on Confronting the Challenges of Development, Environmental Management and Peace Building in the Niger Delta: Beyond the Amnesty. Benin, Edo State, Nigeria, July 28-29, 2011,

—. "The SPDC and Sustainable Development in the Niger Delta". *International Journal of Development Issues*, Vol. 7, No. 1, pp.41-55, 2007.

Ibeanu, O. "Affluence and Affliction: The Niger Delta as a Critique of Political Science in Nigeria". Inaugural Lecture of the University of Nigeria, Nsukka, delivered on February 20, 2008

Ibeanu, O. and Luckham, R. *Niger Delta: Political Violence, Governance and Corporate Responsibility in a Petro-State*, Abuja: CCD, 2006.

Ibrahim, J. "Transforming Elections in West Africa into Opportunities for Political Choice", Keynote Address, Nordic Africa Institute Conference on Post-Conflict Elections in West Africa: Challenges for Democracy and Reconstruction. Accra, Ghana, May 15-17, 2006.

IDEA. *Democracy in Nigeria.* Stockholm; International IDEA, 2000.

IDS (Institute of Development Studies). "From Consultation to Influence: Bringing Citizen Voice and Client Focus into Service Delivery", Brighton, England: DFID Consultancy Report, IDS, 2001.

Ifesinachi, K. & Ezirim, G.E. "Transparency and Governance: A Focus on the Nigerian Extractive Industries Transparency Initiative (NEITI) and the Nigerian Oil Sector". *Nigerian Journal of Humanities and Social Sciences*, (1)2, 2009.

Iheduru, N.G. "Women Entrepreneurship and Development: The Gendering of Microfinance in Nigeria". Paper presented at the 8th International Interdisciplinary Congress on Women, Makere University, Kampala, Uganda, July 21-26, 2002.

Ihonvbere, J. O. "The Nigerian State As Obstacle to Federalism: Towards A new Constitutional Compact for Democratic Politics". In Gana, A. T. and Egwu, S.G. (eds) *Federalism in Africa,* Trenton, NJ08607, Asmara, ERITREA: Africa, World Press, Inc, 2003

—. "Reconstructing the State: Constitutionalism as Public Policy in Africa". In *Agenda Setting and Public Policy in Africa.* Kalu, E.A. (ed). England: Ashgate Publishing, 2004.

Ikelegbe, A., "Governance Deficits and Subsisting Underdevelopment: Rethinking the Niger Problematic". Paper presented at International Development Research Council (IDRC), Think Tank Initiative (TTI) & Center for Population and Environmental Development (CPED) Workshop on Confronting the Challenges of Development, Environmental Management and Peace Building in the Niger Delta: Beyond the Amnesty. Benin, Edo State, Nigeria, July 28-29, 2011.

Ikporukpo, C.O. "Debating Petroleum and Environmental Justice in the Niger Delta: Stakeholders' Perspectives". Monograph Series, No. 1. Centre for Ethnic and Conflict Studies (CENTECS), University of Port Harcourt, Nigeria, 2011.

Ikubaje, John, *Corruption and Anti-Corruption: Revenue Transparency in Nigeria's Oil Sector.* Lagos: Joe-Tohalu and Associates. 2006

Imoobe T. and Iroro T. "Ecological Restoration of Oil Spill Sites in the Niger Delta, Nigeria". *Journal of Sustainable Development in Africa* 11(2): 55, 2009

International Crisis Group (ICG). "The Swamps of Insurgency: Nigeria's Delta Unrest". ICG Africa, 2006.

Jacobson, J.S. "Effect of Acidic Aerosol, Fog, Mist and Rain on Crops and Trees". *Phill. Trans. Roy. Soc. Lond.* B 49: pp. 327-338, 1984.

Jacobs, Davina. "A review of capital budgeting practices". IMF working paper WP/08/160 .Washington, DC: International Monetary Fund, 2008.

Jeffrey J. Lee, Grady E. Neely, Shelton C. Perrigan and Louis C. Grothaus. "Effect of simulated sulphuric acid rain on yield, growth and foliar injury of several crops." *Environmental and Experimental Botany*. Vol. 21(2), p 171-185, 1981.

Joab-Peterside, S. "On the Militarization of Nigeria's Niger Delta: The Genesis of Ethnic Militia in Rivers State". *African Conflict Profile*, Vol.1, No.2. October, 2005.

—. "State and Fallacy of Rehabilitation of 'Repentant Militants' in Nigeria's Niger Delta: Analysis of first phase of the Federal Government's Amnesty Programme". *Pan African Social Science Review*, No. 11, 2010, p.94, 2010.

Kapp, K. *The Social Cost of Private Enterprise*. Cambridge, MA: Harvard University Press, 1950.

Karl, T.L. "Understanding Resource Curse". In *Covering Oil: A Reporter's Guide to Energy and Development*, New York: Open Society Institute, 2005.

Kasum, A.S. "Environmental Degradation Problems Caused by Human Activities in Nigeria: Enforced (taxation) versus Voluntary (Social Responsibility) Solution". *International. Journal of Banking, Accounting and Finance,* 2(3): 1-4, 2010.

Kiss, A. and Shelton, D. *International Environmental Law*. New York: Transnational Publishers Inc., 2000

Kreager, Roland. "Right Sharing of World Resources (RSWR), Fourth Quarter". Vol. XXXVI, No. 4, 2009.

Le Billion, P. "The Political Ecology of War: Natural Resources and Armed Conflicts". *Political Geography,* Vol. 20, PP. 561 – 584, 2001.

Lele, S. "Sustainable Development: A Critical Review", 19 *World Development* 6, 607-621, 1991.

Lele, U. *The Strategy for Economic Development*. Baltimore: John Hopkins University Press, 1979.

Leschine, T. M.; McGee J.; & Gaunt, R. *Federal on-scene Coordinator's report T/V* Exxon Valdez *Oil Spill*. Vol. I. Springfield, VA: Department of Transportation, 1993.

Lippmann, M. "Airborne acidity: estimates of exposure and human health effects". *Environmental Health Perspectives*, 63: 63-70, 1985.

Luong, P.J. & Weinthal, E. "Rethinking the Resource Curse: Ownership Structure, Institutional Capacity, and Domestic Constraints". *Annual Review of Political Science*, Vol. 9, June 2006.

Mabogunje, A.L. *The Development Process: A Spatial Perspective*. Huchington: University Library for African Publications Ltd, 1980.

Madu, I.A. "The Underlying Factors of Rural Development Patterns in the Nsukka Region of South-Eastern Nigeria". *Journal of Rural and Community Development*, 2007 (2), 110 – 122.

Mahler, A. "Nigeria: A Prime Example of the Resource Curse? Revisiting the Oil-Violence Link in the Niger Delta", *GIGA Working Papers*, No. 120, January 2010.

Maloney, W.F. "Innovation and Growth in Resource Rich Countries". Central Bank of Chile Working Papers No. 148, February 2002.

Malthus, T. *An Essay on the Principle of Population as it Affects the Future Improvement of Society (1st edition)* London: 1798.

McGaffey, J. "Initiatives from Below: Zaire's Other Path to Social and Economic Restructuring." In *Governance and Politics in Africa.* G. Hyden and M. Bratton (eds.). Boulder, Co: Lynne Rienner Publishers. pp. 243-262, 1992.

McGinnis, M. D. *Polycentric Governance and Development: Readings from the Workshop in Political Theory and Policy Analysis*. Ann Arbor: The University of Michigan Press, 1999.

Moffat, D. and Linden, O. "Perception and Reality: Assessing Priorities for Sustainable Development in the Niger River Delta". 24 *Ambio* 7-8, 1995.

Moser, C.O.N. *Gender Planning and Development: Theory, Practice and Training*, London: Routledge, 1998.

Munro, D. "Sustainability: Rhetoric or Reality". In *A Sustainable World: Defining and Measuring Sustainable Development.* T. Trzyna (ed.), Sacramento: IUCN, 1995.

Munslow, B. & Fitzgerald, P. "South Africa: the sustainable development challenge". *Third World Quarterly*. 15 (2): 227-242, 1994.

Naanen, B.B.B., "Oil Producing Minorities and the Restructuring of Nigerian Federalism: The Case of the Ogoni People". Journal of CommonWealth and Comparative Politics, Vol. 33, 1995.

Nafziger, W. "Nigeria's Economic Development and Niger Delta Grievances". Conference Proceedings, International Conference on the Nigerian State, Oil Industry and the Niger Delta, Organized by the Department of Political Science, Niger Delta University, in Collaboration with the Centre for Applied Environmental Research, Department of Geosciences, University of Missouri, Kansas City, USA, March 11-13, Yenagoa, Bayelsa State, Nigeria, pp147-156. 2008.

National Bureau of Statistics (NBS). "Nigerian Poverty Profile Report 2010". NBS, Press Briefing by Dr. Yemi Kale—the Statistician-General of the Federation/Chief Executive Officer—National Bureau Of Statistics, held at The Conference Room, 5th Floor, NBS Headquarters, Central Business District, Abuja On Monday, 13th February, 2012.

Niger Delta Citizens Budget Platform. *Budget analysis brief—Rivers State*. Port Harcourt: Niger Delta Citizens Budget Platform, 2009. WWW.citizensbudget.org

NDDC (Niger Delta Development Commission) Act (2000), Federal Ministry of Information and Communications. Abuja: 2000.

NDTCR (Niger Delta Technical Committee Report) . Submitted to the Nigerian Government in November, by the Niger Delta Technical Committee, November 2008

Neufeld, H.S.; J.A. Jernstedt & Haines, B.L. "Direct Foliar Effects of Simulated Acid Rain. I. Damage, Growth and Gas Exchange". *New Phytologist,* Vol. 99, No. 3, pp. 389-405, 1985.

Nigerian Environmental Study/Action Team (NEST). *The Challenge of Sustainable Development in Nigeria*. Ibadan Intec Printers Ltd., 1992.

Nnoli, O. *Path to Nigerian Development*. Dakar: Codeesria, 1981.

Norgaard, R. 'Sustainability of the Economics of Assuring Assets for Future Generations', World Bank, Asia Regional Office, Working Paper Series No. 832. 1992

NPC (National Planning Commission). *National economic empowerment and development strategy*. Abuja: NPC, 2005.

NPC. *National population and housing census,* Abuja: National Population Commission, 2007.

Nwabueze, B. *How President Obasanjo Subverted Nigeria's Federal System*. Ibadan: Gold Press Ltd., 2007.

Nwachukwu, I. N. & Ezeh, C.I. "Impact of Selected Rural Development Programmes on Poverty Alleviation in Ikwuano LGA, Abia State, Nigeria". *African Journal of Food Agriculture Nutrition and Development* 7 (5), 2007. http://www.ajfand.net/Issue16/PDFs/Nwachukwu_2245.pdf (Accessed 16/10/2010).

Oakerson, Ronald J. "Erosion of Public Goods: The Case of Coal-Haul Roads in Eastern Kentucky." In *Research in Public Policy Analysis and Management,* Vol. 2. John P. Crecine (ed), Greenwich, Conn.: JAI Press, pp. 73-102, 1981.

—. "Analysing the Commons: A Framework." In *Making the Commons Work: Theory, Practice and Policy*. Bromley, Daniel W. (ed.). San Francisco: Institute for Contemporary Studies. pp. 41-59, 1992.

Obi, Cyril. "Nigeria's Niger Delta: Understanding the Complex Drivers of Violent Oil-related Conflict". *Africa Development,* Vol. XXXIV, No. 2, pp. 103-128, 2009

Obi, Cyril. "Oil Extraction, Dispossession, Resistance, and Conflict in Nigeria's Oil-Rich Niger Delta". *Canadian Journal of Development Studies* 30, nos. 1–2, 219-236, 2010.

Ogon, P. "The Real Price of Oil: Human Rights Violations in the Niger Delta". Paper presented at the Workshop in Political Theory and Policy Analysis, Indiana University, Bloomington, USA, Friday. October 14, 2005 (Special Session).

Ogunkoya, O.O. & Efi, E.J. "Rainfall Quality and sources of Rainwater Acidity in Warri Area of the Niger Delta, Nigeria". *Journal of Mining and Geology*. Vol. 39(2): 125-130, 2003.

Okaba, Benjamin O. *Petroleum Industry and the Paradox of Rural Poverty in the Niger Delta*. Benin City, Nigeria: Ethiope Publishing Corporation, 2005.

—. "Petrodollar, the Nigerian State and the Crises of Development in the Niger Delta Region: Trends, Challenges and the Way Forward." Unedited conference proceedings, International Conference on 'The Nigerian State, Oil Industry and the Niger Delta,' 21-39. March 11-13, in Yenagoa, Bayelsa State, Nigeria. Port-Harcourt: Harey Publications Company,2008.

Okecha, S.A., Pollution and Conservation of Nigeria's Environment. Ekpoma T' Nigeria Afriqu Inter Ass W.A. Publishers, 2000

Okereke, C. "Insecurity and Power Outages are Significant Drawbacks, but Niger Delta Development Master Plan offers hope for Projects & PM in Nigeria". PM World Today, Vol. IX, Issue IV - April 2007. http://www.pmforum.org/library/RegionalReports/2007/PDFs/Okereke-4-07.pdf

Okoko, K.A.B, Nna, N.J & Ibaba, S.I. *The Politics of Oil and the Underdevelopment of Underdevelopment in the Niger Delta*. Port Harcourt: University of Port Harcourt Press, 2006.

Okonta, I. *When Citizens Revolt: Nigerian Elites, Big Oil and the Ogoni Sruggle for Self-Determination*. Asmara, Eritrea: Africa World Press, Inc. 2008.

Okorodudu-Fubara, M. *Law of Environmental Protection: Materials and Text.* Ibadan: Caltop Publications (Nigeria) Limited., 1988.

Okotoni, M.O. & Akinola, S.R. "Governance of Nigeria's Villages and Cities: Case Studies of Ifetedo and Olode Communities". *African Journal of Institution and Development* (AJID), Ile-Ife. Vol. 2, No. 1, pp. 70-81, 1996.

Okotoni, M. O. & T. A. Akinola. "The Role of Women's Organisations on Grassroots Development in Ife North and Ife Central Local Government Areas of Osun State, Nigeria." *African Journal of Gender and Development*. Centre for Social Policy and Studies, Obafemi Awolowo University, Ile-Ife (ISSN: 2006 - 2192). Vol. 1, No. 1, 2008, pp. 33-43, 2008.

Okwechime, O. "Women's Empowerment, Equality and Development." In *Women and gender Inequality for a Better Society in Nigeria.* Ojo Afolabi (ed.). Leaven Club International, pp. 202-216, 2002.

Olatunbosun, D. *Nigeria's Neglected Rural Majority*. Ibadan: Oxford University Press, 1975.

Olayiwola, L.M. & Adeleye, O.A. "Rural Infrastructural Development in Nigeria: Between 1960 and 1990—Problems and Challenges". *Journal of Social Sciences* 11 (2): 91, 2005.

Olobaniyi, S.B. & Efe S.I. "Comparative Assessment of Rainwater and Groundwater in the Oil Producing Area of Nigeria: Environment and Health Implication". *Journal of Environmental Health*, 6(2), pp 111-117, 2007.

Olobaniyi, S.B. & Owoyemi, F.B. "Quality of Groundwater in the Deltaic Plain sands Aquifer of Warri and Environs, Delta State, Nigeria Water Resources". *Journal Nigerian Association of Hydro geologist* 15: 38-45, 2004

Olowu, D.; Ayo, S.B. & Akande, B. (), *Local Institutions and National Development in Nigeria, Obafemi.* Ile-Ife: Awolowo University Press, 1991.

Olumati, J.C. *Contemporary Human Psychology* (2d ed). Port Harcourt: Peerafi Publications, 2006.

Omo-Irabor, Omoleomo Olutoyin; Olobaniyi, Samuel Bamidele; Oduyemi, Kehinde; & Akunna, Joseph. "Surface and groundwater water quality assessment using multivariate analytical methods: A case study of the Western Niger Delta, Nigeria". *Physics and Chemistry of the Earth* 33: 666-673, 2008.

Omotola, J.S. , "Liberation Movements" and Rising Violence in the Niger Delta: The New Contentious Site of Oil and Environmental Politics, Studies in Conflict & Terrorism, Vol.33, No. 1, 2010, pp.36-54

OMPADEC Quarterly Report. Vol. 1, No, 1, 1993.

Onianwa, P.C; Odukoya O.O; & Alabi H.A. "Chemical composition of wet precipitation in Madan, Nigeria". *Bulletin of the Chemical Society of Ethiopia.* 16(2), pp 41-147, 2002.

Onimode, B. *Africa in the World of The 21st Century,* Ibadan: Ibadan University Press, 2000.

Onuoha, F. C. "The Transformation of Conflicts in the Niger Delta". In *Nigeria Beyond 2007: Issues, Perspectives and Challenges.* H.A.

Saliu, I.O. Taiwo, R.A. Seniyi, B. Salawu, and A. Usman (eds.). Ilorin: Faculty of Business and Social Sciences, University of Ilorin. 2008

Onuoha, F. C. "Corruption and National Security: The Three Gap-Thesis and the Nigerian Experience". *Nigerian Journal of Economic & Financial Crimes*, Vol. 1, No. 2, pp.1-13, 2009.

—. "Youth Unemployment and Poverty: Connections and Concerns for National Development in Nigeria". *International Journal of Modern Political Economy*. Vol. 1. No. 1 (2010), pp. 115-136, 2010.

—. "Proto-Insurgency and Oil Terrorism in the Niger Delta: Implications for the Security of Nigeria's Strategic national Oil Infrastructure". Paper presented at the 2nd International Conference on Natural Resource, Security and Development in the Niger Delta, organized by the Department of Political Science Niger Delta University, at the Niger Delta Wetlands Center, Yenagoa, Bayelsa State, Nigeria, 8-11 March. 2010.

—. "Geo-Strategy of Oil in the Gulf of Guinea: Implications for Regional Stability". *Journal of Asian and African Studies* Vol. 45, No. 3, pp. 369-384, 2010.

Oppong, C. "African Mothers, Workers and Wives: Inequality and Segregation in World Employment Programme". Research Working Papers, Document 2, International Labour Organisation, Geneva, 1987.

Opukri, C.O. and Ibaba S.I. "Oil Induced Environmental Degradation and Internal Population Displacement In Nigeria's Niger Delta", *Journal of Sustainable Development in Africa*, 10(1): 180- 185, 2008.

Osaghae, E., Ikelegbe, A., Olarinmoye, O., & Okhomina, S. "Youth Militias, Self Determination and Resource Control Struggles in the Niger-Delta Region of Nigeria". Research Report, Consortium for Development Partnership Module 5, 2007.

Ostrom, E. *Crafting Institutions in Self-Governing Irrigation Systems*, San Francisco: ICS Press, 1992.

—. "The Rudiments of a Theory of the Origins, Survival and Performance of Common-Property Institutions." In *Making the Commons Work: Theory, Practice and Policy*. Bromley, Daniel W. (ed.). San Francisco: Institute for Contemporary Studies. pp. 293-318, 1992.

—. *Understanding Institutional Diversity*. Princeton: Princeton University Press, 2005.

Ostrom, Elinor, & James Walker (eds.). *Trust and Reciprocity: Interdisciplinary Lessons from Experimental Research*. New York: Russell Sage Foundation. 2003

—. *Governing the Commons: The Evolution of Institutions for Collective Action*. New York: Cambridge University Press, 1990.

Ostrom, V. *The Intellectual Crisis in American Public Administration.* Rev. Edition. Alabama: University of Alabama Press, 1974.

Osuji, L. C. & Ukale, E. E. *Post-oil Spill Fire at Ugbomro (Niger-Delta): A New Vista in Soil-Pollution Studies.* Port-Harcourt: Petrolum Chemical Research Group, 2000.

Pearce, D. and Watford, J. *World without End.* Washington, DC: Oxford University Press, 1993.

Pigou, A. *The Economics of Welfare.* London: Macmillan, 1932.

Priscolli, J. "Participation and Conflict Management in Natural Resource Decision-Making". In *Conflict Management and Public Participation in Land Management.* B. Sohlberg and M. Saija (eds. European Forest Institute (EFI) proceedings 14, 61-88. 1997.

Rajamani, L. "From Stockholm to Johannesburg: The Anatomy of Dissonance in the International Environmental Regime" 12 *RECIEL* 1, 2003.

Rangley, R. "International River Basin Organization in Sub-Saharan Africa". Technical Paper 250. Washington, DC: World Bank, 1994.

Rawls, J. *A Theory of Justice.* Oxford: Clarendon Press, 1971.

Raymond, K. and Coates, A. *Guidance on EIA: Scoping.* Report Number 115, 3 August 2001. Edinburgh: Environmental Resources Management, 2001.

Rivers State Government. *Annual budget estimates.* Port Harcourt: Rivers State, Nigeria, 2009.

Roberts, F.O.N. "Managing the Minorities and Development problems in the Nigerian Federalism". The OMPADEC Initiative, Niser Monograph Series No. 11. Ibadan: Niser, 1998.

—. *Federalism, Hegemony and Petroleum in Nigeria's Political Economy.* Niser Monograph Series No. 3. Ibadan: Niser. 2004

Rodney, W. *How Europe underdeveloped Africa*, Enugu: Ikenga Publishers, 1972.

Ross, M. "The Natural Resource Course: How Wealth can make you Poor". In *Natural Resources and Violent Conflict: Options and Actions.* Banon, I. and Collier, P. (eds.). Washington, DC: The World Bank, 2003.

Rosser, Andrew. *The Political Economy of the Resource Curse: A Literary Survey.* London: Institute of Development Studies, 2006.

Sachs, J.D. & Warner, A.M. "Natural Resource Abundance and Economic Growth". National Bureau of Economic Research Working Paper, No. 5398, 1995.

Sachs, J.D. & Warner, A.M. "The Big Push, Natural Resource Booms and Growth". *Journal of Development Economics*, Vol. 59, 1999.

Sachs, J.D. & Warner, A.M. "Natural Resource Intensity and Economic Growth". In *Development Policies in Natural Resource Economies.* Meyer, J. et al (eds.). Cheltenham: Edward Elgar, 1999.

Sachs, Jeffrey D. *The End of Poverty: Economic Possibilities for Our Time.* New York: Penguin Books, 2005.

Sachs, W. "Environment and Development: The Story of a Dangerous Liaison", 21 *The Ecologist* 6, 1991.

Samuel, K. *Stakeholder Profiles and Dynamics in the Niger Delta: An Options analysis paper on NGOs and other potential development partners.* 2008. http://www.kayodesamuel.com/terrachev.pdf (Accessed February 10, 2009).

Sanda, A.O. *Essays in Public Administration.* Ibadan: Fact-Finders International, 1991.

Sani, H.A. *Public Policy Analysis: Theoretical and Applied Approaches.* Okene; Desmon Tutu Publishers, 2008.

Sawyer, A. *Beyond plunder: Toward democratic governance in Liberia.* Boulder, CO: Lynne Rienner, Inc., 2005

Sawyer, T. "Preparing for Sunset in the Oil Fields". Tell Magazine, February 18, pp. 111-115, 2008.

Selolwane, O.D. "Gender and Democracy in Botswana: Women's Struggle for Equity and Political Participation" in *The State and Democracy in Africa.* Nzongola-Ntalaja, G. and Lee, M. C. (eds.). Harare: African Association of Political Science (AAPS), Zimbabwe, pp. 24-40; 210-217, 1997.

Shah, H. and Goss, S. (eds). *Democracy and the Public Realm.* London: Compass in Association with Lawrence and Wishart, 2007.

Shell Petroleum Development Corporation (SPDC). *Nigeria: Brief note on the Environment and Community Relations*, May 1995

Sills, David L. "Voluntary Associations: Instruments and Objects of Change". Human Organization, 18(1):17-21, 1959

Smith, J. "Imperial Oil", http://indybay.org/newsitems/2006/10/02/18317358.php [accessed 21 October 2006].

Smock, Audrey. *Ibo Politics: The Role of Ethnic Union in Eastern Nigeria.* Cambridge, MA: Harvard University Press, 1971.

Soludo, C.C. "Can Nigeria be the China of Africa?" Being the text of a lecture delivered at the Founder's day of the University of Benin, Benin City, Nigeria, November 23, 2006.

SPDC (Shell Petroleum Development Company). Overview of SPDC Operations, presentation made at SPDC oil seminar for Academics, Port Harcourt, November 5-62008.

Stærdahl, J., Schroll, H., Zakaria, Z., Abdullah, M., Dewar, N., and Panich, N. (2003) "Environmental Impact Assessment in Thailand, South Africa, Malaysia and Denmark". Working Report, 2003. www.ruc.dk/upload/application/pdf/9c4d310e/workingpaper1.pdf (Accessed 12 June 2005).

Stiglitz, J.E. "Making Natural Resources into a Blessing Rather than a Curse". In *Covering Oil: A Reporter's Guide to Energy and Development*, New York: Open Society Institute, 2005.

Tabifor, Christian Phuebong. "BAKASSI Dispute: What an Eye Opener with Its Human Security Threats..." In *Inspire. Network of African Youths for Development*, Yaoundé, Cameroon, August, No. 26. pp. 4-5, 2009.

Tamuno, O.S. *Rural development in Rivers State: An effective approach*, Port Harcourt: Paragraphics, 2009.

Tamuno, T.T. "The Geographic Niger Delta". Conference Proceedings, International Conference on the Nigerian State, Oil Industry and the Niger Delta, Organized by the Department of Political Science, Niger Delta University, in Collaboration with the Centre for Applied Environmental Research, Department of Geosciences, University of Missouri Kansas City, USA, Yenagoa, Bayelsa State, Nigeria, March 11-13, 2008, pp. 916-930, 2008

Tell Magazine..'50 Years of Oil in Nigeria'. February 18, 2008.

—. 'Oil and Development'. February 18, 2008

The Willink Commission Report. *Report of the Commission Appointed to Enquire into The Fears of the Minorities and the Means of Allaying Them*. Presented to Parliament by the Secretary of State for the Colonies, July 1958.

Titilola, S.T. "Environment and Sustainable Agricultural Development in Nigeria". *Journal of Sustainable Development in Africa*, 2 (1), 2000. http://www.jsd-africa.com. (Accessed 20/09/2010.)

Udom, T. "Public health expenditure and social indicators in Nigeria, 1980 to 2005". Port Harcourt: University of Port Harcourt, Unpublished MSc thesis, 2007

Ukiwo, U. *Causes and Cures of Oil-Related Niger Delta Conflicts*. Policy Notes. Upsala, Sweden: Nordic Africa Institute, 2009.

UNICF. *Millennium Development Goals: Combat AIDS/HIV, Malaria, and other Diseases*. New York: United Nations Children's Fund, 2005.

UNDP (United Nations Development Programme). *Human Development Report 2009*. New York: Palgrave Macmillan, 2009.

—. *Human Development Report*. Geneva: United Nations Development Programme, 1995.

—. *Niger Delta Human Development Report.* Garki, Abuja: United Nations Development Programme, 2006.

—. *Niger Delta Human Development Report.* Abuja: United Nations Development Programme, 2006.

—. *Niger Delta Human Development Report.* Abuja: United Nations Development Programme, 2006.

US Energy Information Administration. 'Country Analysis Brief: Nigeria'. http://www.eia.doe.gov/cabs/Nigeria/pdf.pdf

Usman, A. "Re: Nigeria: A nation destroyed by oil wealth". *Daily Trust,* November 11, 2010.

Uwais, M. "Recent Development in Nigeria Strengthening Legal and Institutional Framework for Promoting Environmental Management". Paper delivered at a Global Judges Symposium on Sustainable Development and the Role of Law held in Johannesburg, Republic of South Africa August 18-20, 2002.

Uyigue, E. "Climate changes in the Niger Delta". Nigeria: Community Research and Development Centre (CREDC): 1-3, 2007.

Uyigue, E. and Agho, M. "Coping with Climate Change and Environmental Degradation in the Niger Delta of South Nigeria". Benin. Community Research and Development Centre (CREDC), 2007

Veblen, T. *The Technicians and the Revolution*, reprinted in The Portable Veblen. New York: Viking Press, 1948.

Washington Trend, 2009. http://www.ofm.wa.gov/trends/default.asp

Watts, M.J. "Petro-Insurgency or Criminal Violence? Conflict and Violence in the Niger Delta". *Review of African Political Economy,* No.114, 637-660, 2007.

Watts, Michael J. "The Rule of Oil: Petro-Politics and the Anatomy of an Insurgency." *African Journal of Development* (AJD), vol. 11, No. 2, pp. 27-56. New York: New York University, 2009.

Webber, D. 'Integrating current and development budgets: a four-dimensional process'. *OECD Journal on Budgeting*, Volume 7, No. 2, 2007.

Weiner, A.; Berg, C.; Gerlach, T.; Grunblatt, J.; Holbrook, K.; Kuwanda, M. , "The Exxon Valdez Oil Spill: Habitat Protection as a Restoration Strategy'', Restoration Ecology, Vol. 5,No. 1, 1997,pp. 44-45

Williams, G. *States and Society in Nigeria.* Idanre: Afrografrika Publishers, 1980.

Winograd, M. 'Environmental Indicators for Latin America and the Caribbean'. In *A Sustainable World: Defining and Measuring Sustainable Development.* Trzyna, T. (ed.). Sacramento: IUCN, 1995.

World Commission on Environment and Development. *Our Common Future.* Oxford: Oxford University Press, 1987.

World Bank. *Health Sector Polices*. 2d ed. Washington, DC: Holdman Publishers, 1980.

—. *The Challenge Of Development: World Development Report.* Washington, DC: World Bank, 1991.

—. *World Development Report*. Washington, DC: World Bank, 1994.

—. *Nigeria: Poverty in the Midst of Plenty: The Challenge of Growth Inclusion*, Washington, DC: World Bank 22-35, 1996.

—. *Poverty and Welfare in Nigeria*. Washington, DC: The World Bank and Federal Republic of Nigeria, 1997.

—. *Attacking Poverty: 2000/2001 World Development Report.* Washington, DC: World Bank, 2002.

—. "What is Empowerment?", World Bank Poverty Net. onwww.Worldbank.org/Poverty/Empowerment. 2003

—. "Country Experience with EITI – Part 1: World Bank Cambodia, Oil and Gas Special Supplement", *Petroleum Sector Briefing Note* (5), July 2007.

World Development Report. *Sustainability Development in a Dynamic World: Transforming Institutions Growth and Quality of Life.* Washington, DC:

World Bank, 2003.

www.dfid.gov.uk/pubs/files/eitiworkshopreportfeb03.pdf;

www.saiia.org.za/occasional-papers/saiia-occasional-paper-no.51-october-2009.html

Yates, Douglas. "Enhancing the Governance of Africa's Oil Sector". South African Institute of International Affairs, Occasional Paper, No. 51, November 2009, www.voltairenet.org/IMG/pdf/Africa's Oil Sector.pdf, accessed on 13/12/2009

Zinn, A. "Theory versus reality: Civil war onset and avoidance in Nigeria since 1960", in Collier Paul & Nicholas Sambinies (eds.), *Understanding civil war,* Washington DC: The World Bank 2005.

CONTRIBUTORS

Rhuks Ako is on the faculty of the University of Hull Law School in the United Kingdom. He can be contacted via e-mail at r.ako@hull.ac.uk

Freedom C. Onuoha is a Research Fellow with the Centre for Strategic Research and Studies (CSRS) of the National Defence College, Abuja, Nigeria. His e-mail contact is chufreedom@yahoo.com

Gerald Ekene Ezirim teaches at the Department of Political Science, University of Nigeria, Nsukka, Nigeria. He holds a Ph.D in International Relations. He can be contacted via e-mail ekenezirim@yahoo.com

Sunday I. Efe is an associate professor of Geography and Regional Planning at the Delta State University Abraka, Nigeria, with specialization in Climatology and Environmental Resource Management. His e-mail contact is efesunday@yahoo.com

A. A. Abotutu is a Lecturer with the Department of Geography and Regional planning at the Delta state university Abraka, Nigeria, with specialization in Urban and Regional Planning. He can be contacted at dr.abotutuabel@yahoo.co.uk

Akinsola A. Agagu is a Professor with the Department of Political Science Ekiti State University, Ado-Ekiti, Nigeria He specializes in public policy and his research Interests include Environment, Emergency Management, Comparative Studies, Political Economy, and Ethnic Studies. His e-mail contact is vicagagu@yahoo.com

Steve Otonye Tamuno is a Professor of Economics at the University of Port Harcourt, Nigeria. He is a Development scholar with specialization in Rural Development. His e-mail contact is std19882000@yahoo.com

Titus Udom is a doctoral student in Development Economics at the University of Port Harcourt, Nigeria. He can be contacted at titus.udom@shell.com

Samson Ranti Akinola lectures at Covenant University, Nigeria. His research interest focuses on 'Policy and Institutional Analysis, Polycentric Development Planning, Community Governance, Environment and Poverty Reduction in Africa. His e-mail contact is srakinola@yahoo.com

Lawrence Isidahomhen is the Chairman/Project Director of Life Water Projects International. A local NGO, working on water and sanitation in Lagos Nigeria. His e-mail contact is lawsidi@yahoo.com

Titilayo Aderonke Akinola lectures at the Department of Political Science, Covenant University, Nigeria. Her research interest focuses on Women in Development and Youth Empowerment in Nigeria. She can be contacted via e-mail at takinola@yahoo.com

INDEX